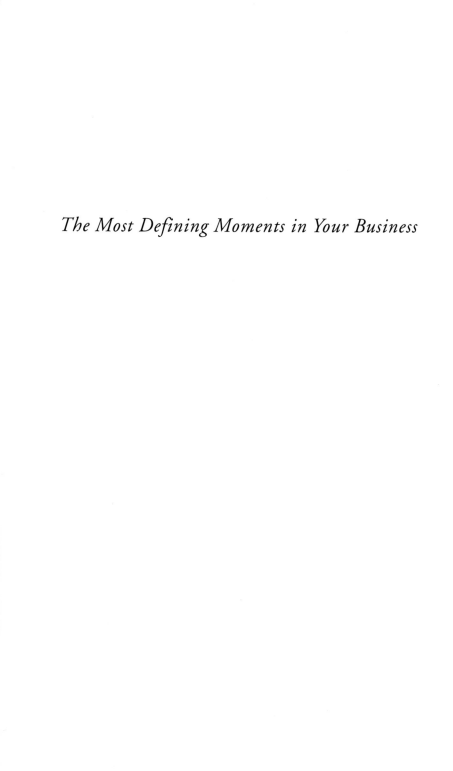

The Most Defining Moments in Your Business

Opportunity Space

Purposeful Interactions
Energizing People,
Producing
Powerful Business Results

By Bridget DiCello

Dedication

This book is dedicated to my dad, Jim Hoffman, my mentor, my teacher and my rock who was the inspiration for this book. Dad is an amazing individual who achieves great things by patiently focusing on others and taking careful action based on what he feels is the right thing to do. By observing his careful focus, I was able to develop the ability to skillfully interact with others. I'm sad to say that as a child and young adult, I argued a great deal with my mom. Despite the arguing, over the years we were able to forge a strong relationship because of the coaching and mentoring from Dad. What seemed like every day of my life after an argument with Mom, Dad would sit with me and we'd talk. He taught me to employ The Three Questions that are a critical part of what I call the Opportunity Space.

Thanks, Dad, for teaching me to interact well with many people important to me and enriching countless relationships as a result. Thank you most importantly for helping me to build a wonderful relationship with Mom and for making our final years with Mom so much fun. Thank you, Mom, for teaching me to believe in the bountiful potential of others and the importance of looking at things from others' points of view. Thank you to my sister Sandy, for insights, clarity, laughs and reflections in the writing of this book and always. Thank you to my husband, Vince, for endless encouragement and support, particularly in finally getting this book written! And to my brother, Adam, you're already so talented, I hope this book helps you find even greater success!

Acknowledgement

Thank you to the entire wonderful team at Design the Planet for all the help with the design and creation of this book!

This book may be purchased for educational, business or sales promotional use. For information, please write:
Bridget DiCello, Building Bridges, LLC
5575 Poplar Avenue, Suite 811, Memphis, TN 38119
Or visit: www.BridgetDiCello.com

Designed by Design the Planet, New Orleans, LA
Published in Collierville, TN by Fundcraft Publishing.

ISBN 978-0-615-38833-5

Contents

Introduction

The Opportunity Space is the moment between when someone does or says something and when you respond.

Since I coined the phrase in 2004, I have taught hundreds of business owners and management professionals how to use this very powerful tool to solve a multitude of communication challenges they face that get in the way of becoming more successful.

In each Opportunity Space™ you make a decision about what you will say and do. This book is about using each of those moments of the day well. In order to do so, you have to make a series of decisions. You need to decide:

1. That you want to improve your interactions with others.

2. That you care enough about the people with whom you interact to think about where they are coming from and how they feel.

3. To invest your energy in listening well.

4. To write down your short- and long-term goals and commit to them.

5. To be persistent and believe in yourself enough to continue to work on these interactions.

Once you've made these decisions, then you can start feeling the exhilarating ride of exponential success that you experience from maximizing every Opportunity Space™!

The Downfall of the Successful

Managers who rise to the top and business owners who succeed have several things in common. They possess a strong desire to succeed, unyielding determination, and a clear vision. They are focused on success and are not afraid to work hard to achieve it. They also possess one other commonality that can and will be their downfall if they are not able to overcome it.

They are not necessarily good communicators. Communication is fairly simple, but far from easy. The concepts seem like common sense, yet are challenging to put into practice. Communicating effectively requires some time and key skills. The fast paced manager does not always feel they have time to spare, nor the need to learn these skills. Because the role of the manager is not so much that of an individual contributor, they will accomplish nothing of significance without communicating with their team successfully.

Amongst the thousands of books on communicating effectively, communication tools and tricks, and seminars on how to communicate well, none of it will work unless you can seize the Opportunity Space™. The good news is that even a small increase in effectiveness will provide significant payoff.

None of it will work unless you can seize the Opportunity Space.

How the Book Works

Anything broken down into its parts doesn't seem that daunting. This book takes what it took me years to learn, presents the Opportunity Space™ concept step-by-step and suggests many activities to help you to internalize the concepts and make their use second nature.

Complete the activities, pay attention to what you think and what you do, and recommit daily to making the changes to improve your interactions, your satisfaction and your success. The energy to recommit daily comes from your desire to solve the specific problems you face.

Pick up Your Pen

When you see the pen, it indicates an activity. Stop and take some time to complete it. Jot your notes in the margin or keep a separate notebook. Either way, write something down. One of the longest journeys a thought can take is from your brain to your hand. Take the journey!

Stop and Think

Have you ever? When you see the 'Have you ever?' symbol, it presents an opportunity for you to think about an experience you have had that inspired you, made you feel good about yourself or caused you to experience some of the similar emotions that are being discussed in the paragraph. It's okay to be self-centered to some extent. There is no clearer frame of reference to *you* than *your* experiences – which makes your experiences extremely powerful resources.

To say you care about how someone feels is one thing. To have felt similarly and to be able to empathize means that you can truly understand how they feel emotionally. When you empathize, you go beyond understanding the situation intellectually. Thinking is logical. Feeling is emotional. At each "Have You Ever" symbol, take a moment to think about your experiences, and think about how you were feeling. This will help you to consider how the other person is feeling, which is a cornerstone of the Opportunity Space™ concept.

Examples

◆ You will learn best when you can think of real life examples of different learning points in action. Throughout the book, there are examples of the concepts presented that are notated with a darkened arrow. As you read through the example, think of situations which you have experienced where you can apply the concept being discussed.

Go For It!

If communication is a challenge for you, or if you feel you have the potential to become more effective, using the Opportunity Spaces™ of the day will enable you to make the best decisions possible to improve your communications, and therefore, your results. The book provides exercises to complete to learn the concepts, but changing your behavior only happens with practice. It is up to you to get out and implement the concept. I did. It changed my life, significantly improved key relationships and provided the key to many of the successes that I have experienced. Go for it!

1

Inspiration

My Story

Back in 2004, I participated in a training program in an effort to build my referral business. The participants shared the motivation, the experience or the passion that led them to start the business they owned today. As my turn came around, I really could not think of what led me to do what I do.

Then one day it dawned on me!

Have you ever? Many of my childhood memories include feeling bad about fighting with my mom. I'm not even sure what it was that we would argue about, but I can remember clearly how mad I'd get and how sad I felt when Mom walked away crying. I'm not sure if you have any of these regrets from your childhood – where you hurt your parents and being a child hardly seems like excuse enough for your behavior. Fights with Mom are definitely in that category of memories for me.

I thank God for Dad. Our calm and patient conversations taught me how to approach any situation well. As a child, after each argument I would be sent to my room and Mom often walked off crying. After I had a chance to calm down, Dad would come and speak with me. He'd ask what it was I wanted to do, and then calmly point out that in getting

Mom upset, my chances for getting to do what I wanted were very slim. Then he'd ask where I thought Mom was coming from and why she was saying and believing the things she did. Finally, he'd ask how I thought I made her feel when I spoke to her the way I did. It was quite a few years before I was able to stop in the moment and ask myself those questions before responding to Mom.

Rude Awakening

Despite Dad's coaching, I was far from perfect at interacting with others when I entered the workforce. Being an "A" student did mean that I had a lot of knowledge from textbooks. However, it also meant I was a little too concerned with doing things "by the book." Coupled with my demanding,

I then realized that in order to accomplish anything significant, I needed to discover what makes people tick.

perfectionist personality, at first I was a bit of a nightmare in the workplace. I had all the "As", the awards and the superb resume and still could not get the team to accomplish what I thought they should. People did not want to work under my guidance. Maybe they were all just slackers, but they responded better to others. I was going to figure this out. I refused to give up!

As a perfectionist focused heavily on results, I then realized that in order to accomplish anything significant, I needed to discover what makes people tick. I needed to learn how to connect with them. It was then that I started applying Dad's lessons.

What will it take for *you* to become frustrated enough to want to interact more successfully with others? How aggravated do you need to become doing things yourself because others don't rise to meet your expectations? Maybe you have already reached that frustration level. You probably have now realized how important communication is and just need to make the commitment to yourself and others that you are ready to learn how to be even more effective.

Once I began to apply Dad's concepts, I realized just how enjoyable it was to interact successfully with others, to help them to achieve what was most important to them and to succeed as a team as well. Now, I firmly believe that in order to accomplish anything, whether mundane or ambitious, people, you included, must feel engaged, excited, involved, important and appreciated.

> *I firmly believe that in order to accomplish anything, whether mundane or ambitious, people, you included, must feel engaged, excited, involved, important and appreciated.*

This book is the result of what I learned on that sometimes painful journey. I spend time working with business owners and professionals to address a variety of challenges, but more than any other strategy, I see the most significant results coming from implementing the Opportunity Space™ concept.

2
Why Use the Opportunity Space?

Michael has always worked hard and been a driven individual. Even from the time he worked in an entry level job, he has had his eye on the senior management positions. He works non-stop 12-hour days, takes work home if he needs to and comes in on weekends to beat a deadline and deliver spectacular results. He lives for exceeding the goals set for him, receives superb performance evaluations and has been promoted three times in the last two years. Michael has also received several major bonuses for his dedication and achievements.

He is eyeing up the Division Manager position. Michael is intelligent, perceptive and learns quickly. He is driven, determined to produce high quality work and expects spectacular results from himself and his team. He sets high expectations from day one with his team, he has some powerful players and they have hit a goal higher than any other team in the history of the company.

But today Michael got some bad news. Chris was getting promoted to the Division Manager position. Michael was crushed! He'd met all his goals, gotten great marks on almost everything in this performance evaluations and he'd been promoted often in the past. He was very upset.

Sensing Michael's disappointment, his boss, Jeremy called him in to his office to have a conversation. Jeremy explained how Michael's contributions to the team and hard work over the years have enabled the company to exceed all expectations.

But he felt that Michael had hit a plateau. Jeremy explained how Michael was going no further up the organization unless he could work more effectively with his coworkers and gain the support of his whole team. He needed to be able to work harmoniously with more than just a few key players on his team and avoid burning bridges.

> *Michael was going no further up the organization unless he could work more effectively with his team.*

Jeremy further explained that because 90% of Michael's performance evaluation scores were top marks, no one had spent much time on his communication challenges. Jeremy told Michael that the harsh truth was that unless he learned how to get others to enjoy working with him, inspire greatness out of "B" players and work effectively with a broad group of coworkers, he was stuck in his current role.

Michael protested that he was working very hard to create a spectacular team. He considered himself a great leader because he was driven towards a clear vision which he had shared continuously with his team.

Jeremy explained that Michael's intense drive for amazing results had led him to push people too hard, fail to listen to their input and not pay attention to their needs. Michael would be judged on the performance of his whole team and could not keep firing people who did not immediately fit and perform to his high expectations. Great leaders, Jeremy explained, communicated with their team members in a way that brought out the best in their capable people.

Are you Frustrated?

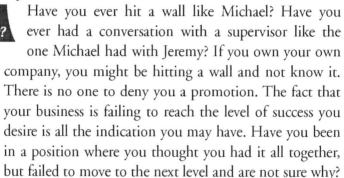

Have you ever hit a wall like Michael? Have you ever had a conversation with a supervisor like the one Michael had with Jeremy? If you own your own company, you might be hitting a wall and not know it. There is no one to deny you a promotion. The fact that your business is failing to reach the level of success you desire is all the indication you may have. Have you been in a position where you thought you had it all together, but failed to move to the next level and are not sure why?

If you're like many business owners and managers, you started a business or got into management because you had a product, skill or ability where you excelled, but you didn't necessarily thrive on interacting with others, especially in stressful

You don't necessarily thrive on interacting with others, especially in stressful situations.

situations. In your business you do not have the luxury of learning as you go along – you don't want your business to wither up while you're trying to become more effective at building and nurturing relationships with all the people who are involved in your business' success.

You may or may not be good at, interested in, or energized by interacting with others. Have you ever been frustrated by:

- Trying to get your point across?
- Getting others to understand your expectations?
- Getting the behavior or response you want from your team?
- Losing your cool, losing your temper, or times when you become impatient or demanding?
- People arguing with you?
- Others constantly challenging you?
- Times when your team is frustrated, annoyed, upset or unhappy?
- Times when they don't respond and don't seem to care?

Becoming more effective at interacting with others could make your business exponentially more successful. Business owners and managers are typically very hard-working individuals, and therefore their businesses will continue to grow and improve, but it can be a long road and a lot of work to make a small jump. You'd probably prefer to have the growth displayed in the graph in Year 2 than in Year 1. Year 2's exponential growth and success comes from finding and implementing something significant which helps the business to *jump* forward. Seizing the Opportunity Space™ in your interaction with others is like fitting the final small pieces of a 2000 piece puzzle into place – the result is a complete and perfect picture! Even the smallest efforts at increasing your effectiveness in communicating will result in significant mileage forward in whatever you are trying to accomplish.

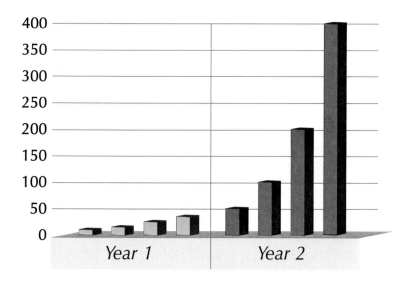

Your Inspiration to Learn and Use the Opportunity Space

One of the most common challenges among business owners and managers is getting others to do what you want them to do. Inevitably in your business you interact with many people, including the employees on your team, your vendors and suppliers, and the customers who sustain your business.

What is your inspiration to learn and use the Opportunity Space™? Maybe you…

- Feel you have more potential in business than you are experiencing
- Desire to be promoted to a senior management position
- Experience frustration in getting your point across
- Have been told by your supervisor you need to improve your communication skills

- Wish to increase your sales significantly
- Would like to increase the enthusiasm of your team
- Believe your employees could take more initiative and you find you lack the ability to get them to do so
- Need to routinely interact with someone who annoys you
- Would like to improve the customer service offered by your organization
- Want to increase the teamwork within your executive team or your entire staff
- Need to decrease your stress
  - When communicating
  - When delegating
  - When holding others accountable
  - When in conflict situations
- Would like to dread conflict less
- Want to increase your performance evaluation scores
- Want to increase the respect and trust you inspire in your team
- Want to earn significant bonuses which have been just out of reach

You already communicate well enough to get things done on a daily basis. What is it for you that is enough of a problem that you will adopt the concepts of this book and put them into place? What are you trying to fix?

1. _____

2. _____

3. _____

Look at the three reasons that you listed above which will inspire you to begin to use the Opportunity Space™.

Are they really important to you? When you think about these particular interactions, are you worried, frustrated or stressed? If you answered "Yes," then that's good motivation to stop and use the Opportunity Space™ well. These motivations will enable you to recommit daily to getting better at those crucial moments – and *you will* see results.

Opportunity Space

The Opportunity Space is the moment between when someone does or says something and when you respond.

Seizing the Opportunity Space™ helps you to interact effectively with others to accomplish what is important to you in a way that matches your goals and values.

First, you must ask yourself The Three Questions:

1. What do I really want to accomplish in the long term?
2. Where are they coming from?
3. How am I making them feel?

The Opportunity Space™ also requires two crucial aspects are in place:

1. You must have clear goals and values in place to guide your decisions during those moments.
2. You must stop and consciously make a decision about what you will do or say next.

Therefore, Opportunity Space™:

• Provides the opportunity to interact most effectively with others to achieve desired results

- Demands your commitment to *stop* and seize the moment
- Requires that you make a conscious decision based on criteria you set about what you will say and do
- Necessitates you have specific values and goals to use as criteria to make good decisions

Opportunity Space™ is comprised of decision moments. Moments must be seized throughout the day to produce long-term results. You may spend time, energy, analysis, committee meetings, and conversations with mentors to make some big decisions, but many of your crucial decisions are made in the Opportunity Spaces™ of the day.

Why are these crucial decisions? They're crucial because in these moments, you are usually having a conversation or interaction that affects someone important to you and to your success.

It's About the People

Interactions between two people are mostly about those two people, regardless of the topic of conversation. People's emotions and feelings will always come into play. If you desire to have successful relationships and successful interactions, then you must take ownership of a situation. You must do this in a way that shows you care about the other person and are thinking beyond satisfying your current emotional needs (which might include the desire to be right, to be defensive, or to avoid fear).

Relationships are built and destroyed, employees are inspired or demoralized, customer relationships are enhanced or hurt, and prospects become clients or are lost – all because of the decisions that are made during the Opportunity Spaces™ of each day.

Think about a time when someone said something to you that really made you feel mad, or sad, or frustrated – I mean *really* frustrated. If any of these memories are from long ago, do you still hold on to them? Do they involve interactions with someone who you really care about? Did they permanently hurt a relationship? Have you ever had an interaction with someone who you cared about that really threw you out of whack, made you upset and did some permanent damage?

> *Relationships are built and destroyed, employees are inspired or demoralized, customer relationships are enhanced or hurt, and prospects become clients or are lost.*

Have you ever said something that afterward you *really* regretted? Maybe it was something that you could tell hurt the person you were talking to – someone you care about? Do you believe that the incident continues to affect the relationship with that person today?

Often, the only part of a situation that you can control is your reaction to it. You cannot "control" others, regardless of your role. You cannot

> *Often, the only part of a situation that you can control is your reaction to it.*

completely control the environment in which the interaction will take place. And you certainly cannot control how others think and feel.

Using the Opportunity Space™ is far from easy, and it takes ongoing effort. Luckily, the concept is simple. It is most effective when you seize every moment of Opportunity Space™ every day. Since it helps you build a relationship which is a process that takes time, it does not always have short-term rewards, so it may not seem worth the effort. Consider how much of your time is spent interacting with people important to you and your success; and realize that the work you put into improving the effectiveness of your communication by one inch will result in miles of payoff!

The good news is that as you train yourself to think this way, it does get much easier. In fact, it becomes second nature and is a way of interacting with others that takes how they feel into account. Then, they begin to feel committed to what you want to accomplish in the long run, enabling you to create a business that is incredibly successful. If you help people to feel good about themselves, they accomplish more – and if they're on your team, that's good news for you!

▶ *Here's an example:* Ben has a problem. He, like Michael, is a driven, hard-working, results-oriented manager and really enjoys his job, but his assistant, Larry, drives him crazy. Larry repeats everything Ben says, seems to dive into unnecessary details, and takes a long time to arrive at the answer that Ben had 10 minutes earlier. Their relationship is shaky. Ben's impatience comes through, and he thinks this assistant is probably not right for the job. Sometimes, Ben will cut Larry off or hurry him along with a "Yeah, yeah, I've thought of that, let's just get it done." Larry seems stressed and unhappy most of the time, although the quality of his work is pretty good.

 Have you ever been in Ben's shoes? Maybe you had to work with someone who drove you crazy. Although you appreciated their hard work, your styles just did not mesh and you did not enjoy working with them. Maybe you decided to leave that particular job because of your frustration. If you were the boss, you might have even insisted they change their approach or fired them. And most likely you did not see them achieve great things or reach an extraordinary level of performance.

Examining Ben's situation using the Opportunity Space™:

When Ben gets impatient, yells or cuts Larry off, he is emotional and is not using the Opportunity Space™ well. First, Ben needs to realize how critical Larry is to his success and commit to addressing how he approaches Larry in order to become a more effective manager. Ben could benefit from using the Opportunity Space™. To do so, Ben needs to freeze reality for a second, step out of the situation (figuratively), assess the situation and ask himself The Three Questions. He will then make an informed decision on how to respond based on his goals and values. For example, what really is more important to Ben, speed or accuracy? Even if speed is his preference, accuracy may be more important to business results.

Ben asks himself The Three Questions:

(1) What do I really want to accomplish in the long term?

In Ben's initial emotional reaction, he may believe that Larry is just too frustrating to work with and that Larry is wrong for the job. Ben might simply start documenting the poor performance and start the paper trail to fire Larry.

However, Ben might also realize that the quality of Larry's work is pretty good. He may acknowledge that he wants Larry to move more quickly but that accuracy is more important. The problem is really more about Ben finding Larry just plain annoying. Larry seems to understand the job better than a lot of previous employees, and that's valuable to Ben. As a team, they have recently been achieving goals that have been long out of reach. Larry's job really doesn't require that he is able to make decisions on a dime and respond immediately, but speed is just what Ben would personally prefer (which is also important, but may not a deal breaker). What Ben really wants to do is produce accurate and timely work and have a positive and productive working relationship with Larry. Ben knows that as his assistant, a good working relationship with Larry is critical to both their abilities to produce quality work.

(2) Where is Larry coming from?

When Ben thought back to the behavior assessments they had done a while ago as a team, he remembered that Larry's results described Larry as detail-oriented, careful, and not prone to make rash decisions. In fact, the assessment also described Larry as someone who needs to talk through things in order to really understand them and someone who works best when he patiently moves through the process slowly and deliberately. Therefore, Ben realizes that if he can create a situation where Larry feels comfortable, Larry will be able to deliver his best quality work. Ben concludes that he can help Larry to be most happy and productive if Larry is given the time to be careful and deliberate about his work.

(3) How am I making Larry feel?

Ben knew that their interactions left Larry feeling as if he was not doing a good job. Ben knew the stress weighed on Larry who would worry about it for some time. Larry really wanted to make Ben happy but continued to believe that high quality work, not speed, was the way to do that.

What should Ben do? Ben has a demanding, high-speed approach to work that he prefers. Larry has a way of doing things that is comfortable to him. Ben has decided it is important to alleviate the tension present in all their interactions. Since he's concluded that Larry is important to the business' success and that personally, his approach as the manager could be better, he stops and takes a deep breath. Ben revisits the value of accuracy over speed as he thinks through The Three Questions.

For future interactions, he decides to give Larry a heads-up before having an in-depth discussion on a task or client. He asks Larry to be prepared to discuss a topic at a certain time and date. The early notification gives Larry the time he needs to think problems through. During the meeting, Ben's need for speed is taken into account because if Larry has time to prepare ahead of time, he can respond more expediently. As a result, Larry has the opportunity to be accurate because he can spend the time preparing and working through the challenge on his own at his own pace. By changing his approach, Ben has found a way to get his results relatively quickly *and* accurately.

Now, a few weeks later, Larry is happier than ever and producing great results! Ben is shocked he ever considered firing Larry.

If you're like Ben or Michael and have worked hard to get where you are, you don't wish to see your goals and aspirations go down the drain. First realize that communication is the only way that a manager accomplishes anything significant and can ever expect to get spectacular results from their team. Then you need to do something about it.

After reading this book, you will have the knowledge to exact changes in your communication abilities and style. Once you've taken the material in, it is work to understand it, practice it and hold yourself accountable to do something with it. Enlist the help and participation of others. As you finish the book, utilize the suggestions in Chapter 11 to ensure the results you want become a reality.

Crucial Elements:

» If you're like many business owners and managers, you started a business or got into management because you had a product, skill or ability where you excelled, but you didn't necessarily thrive on interacting with others, especially in stressful situations.

» Like Michael, you may have hit a limit in moving up the organization or growing your business unless you can work more effectively with your coworkers and gain the support of your team.

» Relationships are built and destroyed, employees are inspired or demoralized, customer relationships are enhanced or hurt, and prospects become customers or are lost – all because of the decisions that are made during the Opportunity Spaces™ of each day.

» Often, the only part of a situation that you can control is your reaction to it.

» The Opportunity Space™ is the moment between when someone does or says something and when you respond.

» In order to respond well in the Opportunity Spaces™ of the day you need to:

- Consider which interactions are most important to you and your business

- Stop the clock and take time to think before you react

- Clarify your goals and values in order to be able to make an informed decision

- Ask The Three Questions:
  - What do I want to accomplish in the long term?
  - Where are they coming from?
  - How am I making them feel?

- Respond purposefully

- Recommit daily to increasing your effectiveness in the Opportunity Spaces™ of the day.

3
The Possibilities

As a business owner or leader, you interact with a number of groups of people. Effectively using the Opportunity Space™ opens up the possibility of becoming more effective at building and nurturing significantly more powerful relationships with all the people who are involved in your business' success.

You might interact routinely with:

- employees,
- subcontractors,
- customers,
- prospects,
- the public,
- referral sources,
- strategic alliances,
- regulators or auditors and
- vendors, just to name a few.

If you could leverage each one of these relationships your business would be unstoppable!

If you could leverage each one of these relationships your business would be unstoppable!

Employees:
As soon as you hire your first employee, your success or failure is to some degree based on their performance. The good news

is that there is enormous potential in each good employee to achieve greatness under your leadership! The star employees and the fantastic teams are drawn to, if not created by, successful leaders who communicate well.

Have you ever? Have you ever worked with a really fantastic team who appeared to work together seamlessly? Picture the best team you ever worked with. How did they communicate with one another? Think about the top performers who you know or with whom you have worked. How would you like a team full of those people?

Like it or not, your response to everything your employees say or do is observed. You can either react consciously and purposefully or you can react without thinking and get what you get in the form of consequences. Going with your initial gut reaction will never bring you a great deal of success. If you want your business to excel, you must strive to act purposefully during every interaction of every day. When you do this well, your employees will feel good about themselves, be more excited about working with you and act in ways that enable your business to be more successful.

Your business will only be a success if you can learn to connect with them and actively engage your employees in their jobs. You must be an effective coach. You must be able to help employees discover their potential, keep them on track with feedback and discipline as necessary, and get them fully engaged. Effectively using the Opportunity Space™ will enable you to build incredibly strong relationships with your employees.

Also, the way you treat your employees tells them a lot about how they should treat the customers. If you tell employees to treat the customers like gold, to really listen to their concerns and to come up with creative solutions, but when you interact with your employees you don't listen to their concerns, you are not focused on creative solutions and you don't ensure that they feel well taken care of, then your chances of employees treating customers like gold is low.

Your Sales People

If you could take the energy and drive that your sales people possess and add an exceptional ability to interact with prospects, customers and operations team members, imagine how successful they could be! Being able to do well in sales requires not only a lot of courage, but an ability to understand the prospects, while staying focused on meeting their true needs. Regardless of how well the sales person knows your products and services, their ability to listen to the customer and ask insightful questions makes all the difference to the bottom line. That way, in the end, the customer is delighted with the product/service they receive and the strong relationship brings them back to purchase more and different products and services.

Have you ever? Have you ever worked with a really effective salesperson? One that did not complain, commiserate or use all kinds of excuses for why they weren't selling more?

If your sales team was able to effectively use the Opportunity Spaces™ during the sales process, their results could be tremendous!

Subcontractors

Imagine if every one of your subcontractors delivered exactly what you really needed, when they said they would and anticipated your expectations!

 Have you ever worked with a subcontractor who took your business as seriously as you do? Do you have a relationship with a subcontractor about whom you do not worry that they will do the job as promised?

Even if you only use subcontractors temporarily or intermittently, they are still representing you to your customer, either through their work or their interactions. They help you deliver a final product important to your customer. Because they are not official members of your team, you may not pay as much attention to them as you do to your employees, but you may also find if you don't use the Opportunity Space™ to interact well, your biggest challenges may lie in the areas that they fulfill.

Customers

Customers are the best advocates, raving fans, insightful contributors and cheerleaders – when you treat them well. Imagine the strength of your database of customers if every one was extremely happy with their interactions with your team!

 Have you ever had a customer who was a real cheerleader? One who spoke about you to everyone they knew, consistently sent you new "A" clients and who was a joy to interact with?

Is customer service a strength of yours? Do you struggle to see the customer as "right" and wish they would not be so challenging sometimes? Or do you find yourself "giving away the farm" because you believe customers must always be given exactly what they ask for? Are you effective in having conversations with both happy and unhappy customers and building long-lasting relationships? The clarity you have for how you wish your customers to be taken care of guide those Opportunity Space™ moments that occur during interactions with all customers.

Once you learn how to use the Opportunity Spaces™ well, the impact on your customer multiplies with each employee who learns this skill. As the leader, you may have limited contact with the customer directly. Your front line employees have the ability to interact with your customers every day in a way that makes the customers extremely happy and pleasantly surprised! And when you lead by example and use the Opportunity Spaces™ well to interact with the employees and the customers your example teaches your team to take great care of the customer.

Prospects, Strategic Alliances, Referral Sources and the Public

Imagine a buzz about your company among your prospects that would keep the phone ringing with ideal clients! Imagine them describing all the great things they've heard about you. Imagine if they were all ready to sign because of a glowing personal introduction and recommendation from a referral source that brought the two of you together!

 Have you ever had a really positive buzz about your company in the general public? Have you had relationships with strategic partners and referral sources that reliably bring you new business? Are your prospects excited about working with you?

Interacting effectively with the general public, your target customers, your prospects, your customers, your referral sources and potential and current strategic alliances creates the relationships which generate sales and increase your revenue. As a business owner or manager, who you are, what you do and how you interact with the general public contributes to your brand and your company image. The better the image, the stronger the brand, the more you can charge and the higher the profit, which is even more important than revenue to the business owner.

Referral sources and strategic alliances can be a phenomenal source of new business. These relationships must be built and nurtured just like any others and they are worth your time and effort to use the Opportunity Spaces™ to make decisions that will build effective relationships.

You will have critical Opportunity Spaces™ in which to build and enhance your brand. You might miss potential customers if your target market is not clear enough and therefore your interactions are not as focused as they could be. The secret to networking effectively to produce results is to be clear who it is you are looking for, go where they go and be effective at interacting with them. Then when you interact with the right target market, use the Opportunity Spaces™ to respond in ways that build the clarity of your brand message.

Vendors

Vendors have favorite "A" clients too. How could life be different and better if you were on every one of your vendor's "favorite client" lists? What special deals or attention would await you?

Have you ever? Have you ever had a relationship with a vendor that was so solid, you did not worry about whether or not they would do as they promised? Have you worked with a vendor who took really good care of you, was happy to bend the rules just a bit or rush to meet a deadline, without the rush charge?

Vendors are key members of your team. Yes, you are *their* customers, and you can become the demanding customer, but your chances of being well taken care of are better if you nurture those relationships as well as you do the others. When vendors make a mistake or there are challenges, use the Opportunity Spaces™ to make the best decisions in those conversations with them, realizing that you are the customer, but that you also want to have a strong long-term relationship. Some day you will need that vendor to do you a big favor – will they want to do it for you?

Regulators

Imagine if you were never worried about interactions with regulators because your relationships were so solid.

Whether your industry is one that is highly regulated or one that only needs to interact infrequently with business overseers, those interactions can be disruptive and expensive. You may be able to forge decent relationships with those who regulate your business, and by doing the right thing, and interacting well, you may feel very little negative impact. Make sure your whole team is using the Opportunity Spaces™ to ensure that the relationship stays positive. There are regulators with whom you are simply trying to do damage control when you are interacting with them. By using the Opportunity Spaces™ well, you might prevent their impact from going from painful to downright damaging.

Demands on Your Time and Attention

You will prioritize interaction with these groups based on how careful you need to be in your conversations. Every successful business owner and manager is going to be on their best behavior with their customers – the people who pay the bills. You may have a customer service initiative on your goals list for this year, you may have a customer service policy or manual, and you may be looking at how you can expand relationships with your current customers. Customers – you pay attention to them. You're also going to pay attention to the regulators or auditors because they can cost you money, and you often have little ability to argue with them.

As far as employees go, there is some great material written on how they should be put ahead of customers on your priority list because they are the ones who take care of your customers. But if you're like most, you put the customer first and expect everyone on the team to be focused on the customer

Figure out which interactions you consider most critical, and put your energies there first.

as well. As for prospects, you may chase them, beg them, or focus heavily on making a great impression in every way possible. For vendors, you are their customers, so you may not pay as much attention to these interactions.

You only have so much time, energy and focus. Seizing the Opportunity Space™ to have positive and successful interactions takes energy and focus and often requires that you act as if you are on stage. This energy and focus may run out as the day or week progresses. You may be one of the few who strive to treat every person extremely well and realize that so many people can affect your success. Most likely you will put some sort of pecking order in place, and this is important to realize when you are exploring the Opportunity Space™, a concept that will ask you to look at every interaction you have every day. Certain relationships may need more work than others, some may be worth more energy than others, and some may need more work now versus later.

Have you ever? Have you ever actively disregarded an employee's need or complaint as unimportant because a customer's need or want was higher priority? Have you ever ignored a vendor's request or pushed the payment window in order to take time, energy or resources to spend on a customer or on marketing and sales efforts instead?

Given that every business needs to generate revenue and make a profit to be differentiated from a hobby by the IRS, your Priority Scale order might look like this:

_____ 1. **Prospects and the Public** – because they represent new revenue, company growth and exciting new work, and you want the image of your company to be positive

_____ 2. **Customers** – they pay the current bills, the hard work of bringing them in is done and you have an existing relationship with them.

_____ 3. **Auditors** – because they can cost you money, you just try to minimize the loss

_____ 4. **Strategic Alliances/Referral Sources** – because they are a source of potential new business

_____ 5. **Employees** – you are paying them to do the job

_____ 6. **Subcontractors** – you are paying them to do the job and you are not as committed and invested in them as you are in your employees

_____ 7. **Vendors** – you are their customers.

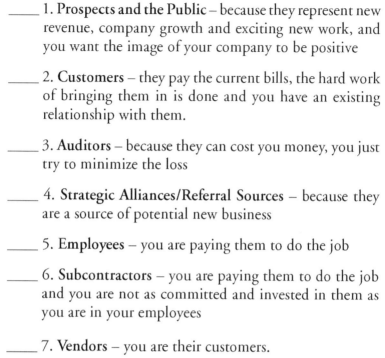

You may or may not prioritize according to the list above. However, when you look at the bottom line that keeps a company functioning, you may make decisions according to the order above even if you see your employees as a very important part of your overall success. Take a moment to rank these groups in the order you would prioritize them in the blanks to the left. Think about if two of these individuals came to you at the same time with a need, who would you take care of first? If you want to be successful, you will take care of them both, but you *will* have to choose which one to take care of first.

Crucial Elements

» Become much more effective at nurturing and leveraging significantly more powerful relationships with *all* the people who are involved in your business' success and your business will be unstoppable!

» Using the Opportunity Spaces™ of the day requires time, energy and focus. Figure out which interactions you consider most critical, and put your energies there first.

4

The Foundation for Making the Right Decisions

You would think that as a results-oriented, focused manager you would have no trouble making good decisions. It is when your determination to succeed involves enlisting the commitment from others and requires your communication to do so, that you might unwittingly deviate from your goal-directed path.

When your determination to succeed involves enlisting the commitment from others, you might unwittingly deviate from your goal-directed path.

When you find yourself in an Opportunity Space™ and faced with a decision of how to react, you will consult certain criteria to arrive at your choice. The criteria may concern emotional needs (such as fear, pride or anger), and if your values and goals are not clearly defined, your decisions will often end up being based on emotions. By clarifying your goals and values and writing them down, you will be able to operate with a clear focus and lead your team cohesively.

Have you ever? Have you ever made a decision you regretted later that was based on emotions in the moment instead of thoughtful awareness of your goals and values? Was it easy to get swept up in the moment? And later, did the decision not make sense when you took into account your goals and values?

Even if you feel as though you are in touch with your values and have goals in your head, unless you have clarified them and put them in writing, they may waiver or be lost among the tumult of emotion.

When values are written, clear and top of mind, they can more easily be used to make decisions in the Opportunity Space™ in an unemotional and expedient way.

Your values and goals may waiver or be lost among the tumult of emotion.

Written Business Goals	+	Established Values	=	Good Decisions for Your Organization in the Opportunity Spaces of the Day

You make decisions in this Opportunity Space™ by combining your business values and your business goals with what you are able to accomplish emotionally and realistically in the moment. The right thing to say and do is rarely black and white. It is more a matter of shades of gray that become more clear when you reference your business values and goals which are written, shared and acted upon.

Values

As a company owner or leader, your business values should be well defined and shared with others in the company. When these values guide management's decisions, a pervasive culture is created throughout the organization. In order to be believable, business values must be consistent over time, across the company's budget, expenditures, and direction and throughout the leaders' actions and expectations.

> *In order to be believable, business values must be reliable over time.*

Even if you're not the business owner, your values still matter! The owner establishes values for the business overall. Then, each leader within the organization bases the values for their department on the business values and adds clarity for their team by establishing how they will get it done in their particular area of responsibility.

How to Define Your Business Values

An initial list of values can be determined using the exercises on the following pages. Your values can be refined over time as you deal with situations and heighten your awareness of how you put your values into practice. Your understanding of your business values expand and deepen over time as you make decisions. When you observe the consequences of how the decisions play out and you observe yourself making

> *If your values are not crystal-clear to you, they will not be able to be acted upon by your team!*

decisions that may appear contrary to your stated values, you can then refine and clarify your values.

If your values are not crystal-clear to you, they will not be able to be acted upon by your team!

Some business values may include:

1. **Innovation** – continuous improvement of processes and products
2. **Consistency** – producing the same dependable results
3. **Reliability** – predictability according to set expectations
4. **Phenomenal Customer Service** – according to your customers' needs and expectations
5. **Accuracy** – precision and details
6. **"Wow" Work** – consistent client response
7. **Cleanliness** – of locations and equipment
8. **Productivity** – maximum utilization of resources
9. **Efficiency** – in planning, production
10. **Punctuality and Timeliness** – as promised, on time
11. **Quality** – function, speed, value, suitability
12. **Responsiveness** – reaction to customer needs, and anticipated needs
13. **Safety** – of products, services, and facilities
14. **Speed** – replies, production, changes
15. **Accountability** – of the team for performance and results
16. **Communication** – proactive, frequent, according to preferences, effective
17. **Cooperation** – among individuals and departments
18. **Competition** – strive to excel, exceed performance levels of the past or of others

19. **Coordination** – seamless interaction of individuals and stakeholders

20. **Discipline** – adherence to policies, procedures, systems, schedules and standards

21. **Risk taking** – ability of employees to take risks, make decisions, and try new things

22. **Systemization** – creation of systems and processes to streamline operations

23. **Professional development** – improvement by all individuals, departments and company as a whole

24. **Creativity** – bright ideas, connecting seemingly unrelated ideas and concepts

25. **Integrity** – doing what you say you will do, behind the scenes as well

26. **Solid relationships** – with employees, vendors, partners

27. **Giving back to the community** – with employee time, donations, projects

Take a moment to circle the values above that you think are the top five values for your organization. Then work through the activities below to confirm or clarify your company values. Although you may believe that all of the above values are important, there are certain ones about which each leader feels most passionate. The ones you circle should be inherent in everything your company does.

Identifying and Clarifying your Values - Exercises

1. What bugs you? Make a list of what bothers you. Include everything from 'slow drivers in the left lane,' to 'employees who don't seem to care the customer is there.' Just write. They don't have to be work related. List 25 things. If you can, make a list of 25 things that bug you in the

workplace and then 25 that bug you outside of the work arena. This task is especially easy on a frustrating or overwhelming day. Then, when you have calmed down a bit, ask yourself *why* these things annoy you. Continue to ask yourself 'Why?' until you get to a root cause. Then ask what this tells you about you to determine your underlying values.

▶ *Here's an example:* It really bothers me when I walk up to a register and the salesperson does not acknowledge that I am there. I could at first assume that is because I don't like to be ignored, I feel hurt she isn't taking time for me, or I don't have the time to wait for her to do her job. However, if I continue to ask why it really annoys me, I will personally come to the conclusion that I believe every person should feel good about themselves and know they are important, and by ignoring me, I conclude she is probably ignoring others. This may make them feel unimportant. That's really why it bothers me, and that value carries over to my interactions with people. When in a leadership role, I will always do my best to take time to give people my undivided attention, make them feel that they are important and what they have to say is important. I want to lead by example so that others in my organization will do the same for each other and for our customers. That begins to create our culture.

 2. Whom do you admire? Make a list of the ten people you admire the most. Then write what you admire about them. They don't have to be famous people or family. They can be the gentleman you see routinely at your favorite coffee shop. They don't have to be people you admire for anything extremely significant either. What you admire about them are things that you value.

▶ *Here are two examples:* I admire Mother Teresa. She was very patient and extremely determined, without any desire to be recognized for her great efforts. She was calm, driven, accomplished a lot, and made a positive difference in the lives of a lot of people who may have thought their situation was hopeless. I admire my mom, because she had a quiet, powerful way of pushing everyone who interacted with her to achieve just that little bit more than they thought they could. They would walk away feeling much better about themselves than before they interacted with Mom.

3. Paint a picture with words of what you want your future to look like. Think unbelievable - make it vivid and exciting and inspiring! Stretch what you believe is possible while making it specific. Describe a destination as well as the values included in the journey to get there.

▶ *Here's an example:* In my imagined future, in 10 years, the delivery of the leadership training programs I've developed will be positively affecting managers and their employees throughout the world. Because of attending my classes, managers will enjoy leading others, be successful at it, be excited to do what they do and be able to do it well. And I will have played a key role in the movement to add practical leadership courses to the curricula of all undergraduate and graduate business programs throughout the U.S. Beyond looking forward to the tasks they will do and the pay they will receive, graduates will look forward to building strong connections with the people with whom they will work at their new jobs. I value helping large numbers of people to be successful, presenting practical and easy to use information, and inspiring others to enjoy leadership.

4. Complete this exercise to determine your business values: You are going on vacation for three months to Costa Rica to enjoy the beaches, the mountains, the white water rafting and the hot springs. The good news is that this is an all-expense-paid trip. The challenge is that you are not allowed to communicate with anyone back at the office. However, you must ensure your company continues to operate how you want it to, so you still have happy customers and employees when you return. What are the five key points you will emphasize to your employees?

If you are tempted to say, "Make good decisions by doing what you think I would do," you must be more specific about how it is you go about making decisions and detail the criteria you routinely use to make decisions.

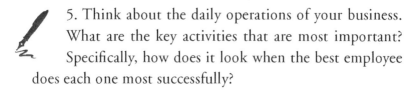 *Here's an example:* Solve the Customer's Problem. They might not always be right, but you are committed to helping them through their challenges. First, make sure you clearly understand the problem. Avoid jumping to conclusions. When you think you understand their problem, ask two more clarifying questions. Give them a specific timeframe in which you will get back to them and live up to that promise. Call on each other for help to come up with a solution that makes them happy while staying within your budgetary limits.

5. Think about the daily operations of your business. What are the key activities that are most important? Specifically, how does it look when the best employee does each one most successfully?

Here's an example: In a retail establishment, as a customer walks in the door, the best employee greets them,

"Good morning, welcome to ABC Store, I'm here to help if you need me."

Customer – "I've got a problem with this product I bought."

Employee – "I can help you. Can you please tell me what happened?"

Customer – "I just bought this yesterday, the clerk didn't show me how to use it, and now I'm really frustrated because I can't get it to do what I need it to."

Employee – "That sounds frustrating. I would be happy to help. My name is Shana – let's sit over here for a moment so I can give you my full attention. Maybe we should start with whichever function is most important to you?"

This employee is demonstrating sincere and consistent values of communication, responsiveness and building relationships.

Clarifying your Values

Once you've completed the exercises, take a few moments to find pervasive values that keep recurring in your work. Then keep that list next to your desk for the next week. Challenge yourself to see how often *you* adhere to each value. Are these values really prominent in all you do? Or have you simply made a list of what you wish your company could be? You rarely adopt a value that is not inherently important to you. Therefore, what you do on a daily basis and how you act and react is a double-check for your list of values. If your list of values is what you *hope* your business would be, then make sure you are working actively to make those values a reality in order to preserve your credibility.

A common value is to reward and appreciate your team members for a job well done. Make sure you genuinely feel appreciation is important and do it right. I've seen too many managers make a big, public deal of what someone has done right, and you can see by watching that the public praise is actually embarrassing the employee. When the praise concerns them having finally taken a small step on something they were struggling with and most of the rest of the team have accomplished this ages ago, it can be particularly embarrassing. For example, a supervisor might announce, "Marty got his report in on time this week!" Make sure your appreciation is genuine, not sarcastic. Give praise privately if it concerns a small but significant step over an obstacle that may be something the individual may not choose to share with colleagues.

Another common value is teamwork. The goal is to solve problems cooperatively, use each other's strengths and compensate for each person's weaknesses. However, if in reality the boss is coming down hard on people who make a mistake and prompting others to find and place blame, it encourages everyone to cover themselves for their own job security. They are being taught that risk is not okay because failure is not okay.

What you consider your values may need to be refined over time.

▶ *Here's an example:* When I was the administrator of a nursing home, as a team we worked with the families of the residents to ensure the residents continued healthy relationships with their families and friends and had visitors to keep them company. Our social services role led us to encourage the families who did not visit. A significant realization struck me as we worked with one particular family. We strongly and repeatedly pushed a reluctant daughter to visit her mother. She finally informed us that if our mother had physically, sexually and emotionally abused us, we wouldn't find it necessary or pleasant to visit her often either! This poignant experience led us to refine our values. Where we once strove to ensure that families visited residents, now we wanted to do our part to create the best experience for both the resident and their family members based on their particular family dynamics. In some cases, it still meant encouraging interaction. Or in other cases, it meant keeping family members posted on progress without requiring them to come by the facility often. We needed to learn about all our customers, both family and residents, and enhance their experience accordingly.

▶ *Here's another example of clarifying values:* One of the managers with whom I worked, the dietary director at the nursing home, really disliked public praise. Every year, we organized and held a luau for our residents, their families and their guests. The dietary department did a really great job on the food. It was delicious, unique and presented creatively and ornately. We purchased a real flower lei and presented it in front of the crowd to the dietary director. The first year I worked with him, he asked that I not do that, and I assumed he was just being modest. The second year we worked together, he insisted and got very serious about not wanting to be pulled up in front of everyone and recognized. He encouraged me to call out his whole staff, but just leave him out of it. So,

I did. The staff really enjoyed the recognition they received, and he was delighted to be left behind the scenes. Little did I know that my recognition publicly of him that first year really annoyed him and did nothing to enhance the relationship and show my appreciation.

Goals

*If you don't know where you want to go,
you'll probably never get there.*

Have you thought about writing or already written a draft of your goals for this year? As a goal-directed, focused and driven person, it may seem like a waste of time to spend a whole lot of effort writing goals that are already very clear to you. Have you ever protested with one of the excuses below?

Top Excuses for Not Writing Goals:

5. They are already in my head, very clearly.

4. I can't predict the future – Who knows what next year will look like in these crazy economic times? I'm just going to keep working extra hard all year like I did last year.

3. If I write them down on paper and don't reach them, I'll have failed!

2. Last year I thrived, so I'm just going to keep doing to same things.

1. Things work best when I go with my gut in the moment.

It is important to have written goals for the company or your department and have shared them with your team – everyone important to the success of your business. Then when you reference them in the Opportunity Space™ in order to make a decision, it won't be the first time the other person has heard them. Share the plan to reach the goals as well.

Revenue is the most frequently written goal. Many conflicts occur not because people disagree about the need to achieve increased revenue but the methods by which to get there. This is why it is so important to write more than just revenue goals.

Goals should also be written in the areas of:

- Operations (improving systems and processes),
- Customer service (enhancing the experience),
- Innovation (improving the product),
- Team (work flow, interactions),
- Marketing and sales (each person's role),
- Professional development (ongoing education, personal improvement),
- Purchases (capital equipment),
- Work environment,
- Any others you find important.

If you don't have goals written in a majority of these areas, try the process below to get it done.

Steps to Write Effective Goals:

1. Write a list of the Top 50 things you most want to accomplish in the next 12 months, including personal and professional aspirations. *This is the hardest part – get it done and you're well on your way.* **Stop reading and at least start this list right now - immediately.** This is not

a list of goals, but rather things you want to accomplish. Writing a book was on my list for years before it moved from this wish list to my goals.

2. Group wish list items into categories of related topics to be able to focus your efforts. You should have some in each of the categories on page 55, as well as in any other categories that might be applicable to your business.

3. Identify the top three items that you are most *excited about.*

4. Choose 5-10 items or groupings which you want to turn into goals. Refine them to be specific and measurable, and have a deadline for completion.

5. Identify and acknowledge the two which will be most difficult to achieve.

6. Break down any 12-month goals into what you need to achieve each quarter and each month in order to reach them.

A majority of business owners do not write a complete list of goals. Many just have a revenue number goal. You don't need to write goals in order to stay in business, but your chances of achieving great success with your business is much better if you clarify your goals enough to write them and you share them with your team.

Most managers don't write goals either. They usually adopt the goals written for them. When this happens, that manager misses an opportunity to act on what they believe is possible rather than simply living up to what someone else says must be accomplished.

> *Here's an example:*

Wish list items:
- Decrease the Chaos – mainly when a key player is out sick or on vacation

- Increase the number of people who know how to do certain tasks
- Increase interoffice cooperation.

Goal: Create a three month schedule of cross-training and half-day department hopping with the explicit purpose of gaining some depth of knowledge for completion of key activities. Create the schedule by May 15th to include a plan for June, July and August. Include responsible parties and progress meetings and deadlines.

Getting Results with Values and Goals – Living the Values

Once you've clarified values and goals, plan to share them strategically, lead by example and encourage them purposefully. It is vitally important that values and goals are shared with other members of your team, including employees, strategic partners, customers and vendors. You'll probably share different goals with these different groups, in varying levels of detail – enough to help them to work with you to achieve the goals, yet retaining confidentiality as appropriate. Values become apparent as employees watch their boss's actions and let the boss lead by example. Goals and values should also be explicitly stated in a mission or values statement and publicized and discussed.

 Leading by example happens whether or not you do it intentionally. Consider how you want your employees to treat each other and treat the customers. Make a list of the top five guidelines important to you in those interactions with other employees and with customers. Then ask yourself how your team learns that that behavior is important. Can they watch you? Do you teach them? Do you reiterate it?

Have you ever? Have you ever worked with a leader who you really admired? What did they do that impressed you? Did those actions match what the leader said? Have you ever worked with a leader who really drove you crazy? What specifically did they do that frustrated you? Did that match what they said?

You can spend a lot of time in orientation and ongoing training to teach your employees your business values, but the fact is that the company values are best learned by on-the-job observation of you, their leader. This means you need to live by your goals and values in each Opportunity Space™. Make decisions in those moments that are in line with your core values in order to teach everyone else how to make those decisions.

Once you define the values and teach them to your team, make sure you publicly recognize when they are demonstrated to encourage that ongoing decisions are made according to this set of values.

Crucial Elements

» You would think that as a results-oriented, focused manager you would have no trouble making good decisions. It is when your determination to succeed involves enlisting the commitment from others and requires your communication to do so, that you might unwittingly deviate from your goal-directed path.

» Even if you feel as though you are in touch with your values and have goals in your head, unless you have defined them and put them in writing, they may waiver or be lost among the tumult of emotion.

» In order to be believable, business values must be reliable over time, consistent across the company's budget, expenditures, and direction and dependable in the leaders' actions and expectations.

» Once your goals and values are crystal-clear to you, then they will be able to be acted upon by your team.

» If you don't know where you want to go, you'll probably never get there.

» Take the time and make the commitment to the goals and values in your head by writing them down and sharing them with all those important to your success.

» When you share the values and goals, you build your support structure. It's much easier to make the right decision and respond well in the Opportunity Space™ when you are surrounded by those who know, understand and buy in to what you're trying to accomplish.

5

The First Question:
What Do You Really Want to Accomplish in the Long Term?

The business environment is very focused on short-term results to measure company success, potential and rewards. However, as you saw in Michael's situation, even record-breaking short term results still limited his ability to personally achieve his goal of being promoted to higher positions. The problem with a short-term focus is obvious since many short-term appearances of success often do not plant the seeds for long-term, sustained results.

Communication that simply communicates your point, with little regard for the integrity of the interaction in the long term can destroy relationships and wear out dedicated team members.

Communication that simply communicates your point can destroy relationships and wear out dedicated team members.

A business owner may be drawn towards taking actions that bring about short-term results because of a desire to see benefit resulting quickly from all their hard work.

However, this focus leads to problems in the long run because long-term success determines the longevity of the company, the return on their investment of time, energy and money, and their risk rewarded. A manager may receive good performance evaluation marks and achieve certain promotions, but their interactions may create a definite ceiling in the organization in the long term.

Have you ever? Have you ever felt pressured to produce short term results, either by your boss or because of the results you wanted to see in your own business? Have you ever disregarded your concerns about long term repercussions because of an urgent need? Did you regret it later and kick yourself for not thinking beyond the present challenges?

Why Think Long Term?

This first question, "What do you really want to accomplish in the long term?" is really important because it asks you to look at how your response in this interaction might come back to either help you or hurt you in the future.

Every conversation either builds or hurts the relationship with the person with whom you are conversing. Make no mistake, each and every conversation affects the relationship positively or negatively. The only acceptable responses from you are those that will strengthen this relationship if this person is in fact critical to your success.

> *Every conversation either builds or hurts the relationship with the person with whom you are conversing.*

When you interact with people, they remember the bad and the good. Unfortunately they usually remember more of the bad because of how you have made them feel.

It is often hard to remove emotions and respond appropriately all the time, but if you stay focused on what you want to accomplish, which is usually building a stronger relationship in order to achieve some business goal, you have a better chance of achieving that.

Thinking Big

In order to effectively think long term, it becomes necessary to take an inventory of what you think is possible. Often, people limit themselves and others because of what they believe they and others are capable of accomplishing.

Over and over, expectations have been proven to determine results. This occurs because your beliefs and expectations determine how you act. It is human nature to not want to be wrong. Therefore, you will act in ways that make your beliefs and expectations true.

> *You will act in ways that make your beliefs and expectations true.*

Whatever you believe to be true, you will see the things that make this true and confirm your beliefs. You will not be on the lookout for other opportunities, you will naysay possibilities that arise because you don't believe they will happen, and you will prove yourself right in the long run.

 Challenge your beliefs and expectations. Make a list of things that you really want. Many times, I have asked the question of business owners, "What do you really want to achieve in your business?" and of managers, "What do you really want to achieve in your department?" They give the standard answers first: meet or exceed current goals, increase sales, lower turnover, deliver better customer service, etc. When continually asked what they really want, most find it difficult to arrive at deeper answers because their brains don't tend to work that way. They have so much to do, and there is little time to think of things that are not realistic and practical.

 In order to Think Big, first make a list of the parameters you believe to be true:

- What do you believe to be true about your industry?
- What are the industry leaders like? Why do they experience greater success than you?
- What is your role as the owner?
- What do you believe about the motivation and potential of your employees?
- How much could your business grow in the next year?

Then, challenge every one of those parameters. Consider them limitations to be overcome. Ask, "What if…?" What if that was not true? What if you were wrong about one of those answers? What is the best possible scenario? What is the best in your industry going to look like in 10 years?

Ten years ago, how many of us envisioned our multi-technology handheld devices that we use today, formerly known as telephones? Okay, if you're a big techie, you probably did. However, you tend to think realistically about your own business. This is because if I told you to think really, really big and then *go for it* – there is that chance you'd take a big risk and lose it all. That's not my advice. But *thinking* big is the first step to getting there.

Have you ever had big thoughts or a bold vision and others thought you were crazy? Have you ever seen big potential but talked yourself out of it because it was unrealistic, and regretted it later because your original insight was correct?

Have you ever?

And thinking big is the first step to using the Opportunity Space™ well, because first you need to have high expectations about those with whom you interact in order to effectively access the potential in each interaction.

▶ *Here are a few examples:* From "Chapter 2 – Why Use the Opportunity Space™?" situations that might be a challenge to you are below with possible long-term big thinking suggested for each.

- If you feel you have more potential in business than you are experiencing, Think Big! Think 200% growth! This big thinking works alongside a goal of 25% growth for example. All your strategies and systems are focused on the 25% growth to ensure it happens, but your thoughts and conversations are conducted in a way that enables the environment and relationships to be created that will support 200% growth.

- If you desire to be promoted to a senior management position, Think Big! Think two positions higher than you think is possible. Chances are, you are currently thinking one position lower than you think possible in order to avoid disappointment. Picture yourself in that higher position and do things, say things and act in ways that fit that picture.

- If you experience frustration in getting your point across, Think Big! Believe you can develop the ability to read each person with whom you interact. Picture yourself understanding what they're thinking and how they might need to hear the information to have it successfully communicated. Believe you can read them effectively, virtually all the time. Thinking this way about your abilities will open your eyes to ways of communicating you may not have thought of if your mentality had been focused on just surviving the current conversation.

- If you have been told by your supervisor you need to improve your communication skills, Think Big! You might at this time prefer to believe that this supervisor is just impossible to please and their standards are too high. But, what if you worked for not only their approval, but their pleasant surprise with your performance?

- If you desire to increase your sales significantly, Think Big! Be determined to top the most anyone has ever sold in a month or year. Believe that you can discover unique ways to find new prospects and innovative approaches to closing the deals. You can develop the exceptional ability to build excellent rapport and strong relationships with any prospect or customer. You will become known as the best sales professional and an expert at cross-selling and expanding relationships with current customers.

- If you would like to increase the enthusiasm and initiative of your team, Think Big! Believe each member of the team will contribute according to their individual strengths at key times, with opportunities for them to participate structured into daily interactions and operations.

- If you need to routinely interact with someone who annoys you, Think Big! Plan to do and say things that create a strong relationship between the two of you where you must rely on each other. Call on each other for help and speak highly of one another even when the other is not present.

- If you would like to improve the customer service offered by your organization, Think Big! Be determined to meet a specific customer need that is currently considered impossible.

- If you want to increase the teamwork within your executive team or your entire staff, Think Big! Picture a seamless, strategic interaction where each member brings forth ideas, researches initiatives, reports to the group, adds intelligent discussion to other's ideas, and speaks with tact and respect for one another. This results in one significant innovation each month, whether it be a new product, or and innovation in operations or sales.

- If you need to decrease your stress, Think Big! Every morning, hop out of bed really looking forward to work. When you think about interactions with key players, feel energized and not worried.

  - When communicating – You find the right words to say, don't feel any negative emotions, and get a good response.

  - When delegating – You effectively explain what you need done, and you follow up appropriately. As a result, tasks get done better than you expected earlier than you asked.

  - When holding others accountable – You find an objective, unemotional way of providing feedback in a way that causes others to want to improve their performance and take responsibility for what they are expected to do.

  - In conflict situations (you'd like to dread it less) – Although most people find it hard to enjoy conflict, you are able to approach it in a way that you look forward to the insights that will result from the conversation. You're ready to admit if you're wrong and ready to let the other person still feel good about themselves even if they happen to be wrong.

- If you want to increase your personal performance evaluation scores, Think Big! Instead of writing off one or two of the categories in which you feel you will never really excel, be determined to bring them all up a notch. Imagine yourself as the expert in the areas you struggle the most. If you were the expert, how would you act?

- If you want to increase the respect and trust you inspire in your team, Think Big! Picture each member of the team understanding your vision, agreeing that it's worth working for, and believing in you. Meanwhile, you believe in all team members, trust them, and have an honest relationship. If something were to happen in which trust or respect came into question, you'd have a great conversation which would allow you to resolve the situation quickly.

- If you want to earn significant bonuses which have been just out of reach, Think Big! Shoot for the top bonus available. If you own your own business, aim for the biggest profit you can picture. The activities in which you engage for each level of reward will be different. When you think about the biggest bonus on the table or profit double or triple last year, your thought processes change for the better.

Why Think Big? Isn't it just being unrealistic? If you can never really expect the level of perfection that is described in the examples above, why think that way? Won't you just be continually disappointed?

Here's an example: According to the scale on page 68, let's say your customer service is currently at a '3.' You can be realistic and think like a '6' believing that there will always be customers who you can't make happy, those who don't fit with your organization and those who will just never be satisfied.

However, if you Think Big, you will interact with each customer believing that you can connect with everyone enough to make them all happy, even if grumping is part of their communication style. If you strive for a '6' and make it two-thirds of the way

> *When you Think Big, you realize results that are above what you felt was realistic!*

there, you're at a '5'. Whereas, if you Think Big and strive to make every customer happy (a 10) and get two-thirds of the way there, you're just above a '7.' And that result is better than you thought was realistic! You'll have connected with a few more key customers and that could have resulted in significantly higher revenue.

10 **Thinking Big** – Connecting with *every* customer, making each one happy

9

8

7

6 **Realistic Thinking** – You'll always lose some, but you will take great care of the majority.

5

4

3 **Where you are** – Way too many unhappy customers.

2

1

Think Big!

Share Your Big Thinking

Share your long-term, big-thinking goals with others. They will tend to act in productive ways if you share the goals in a way that lets them know you care. If they see you have similar goals to their own, if they feel you can relate to them and if they are excited about the destination in which you are both headed they will be much more engaged. How you respond in those Opportunity Spaces™ will determine whether or not you get closer to those long-term goals.

Put a plan in place to share your big thoughts. Incorporate it into:

- interview questions to find people who fit the open position
- goals you set with individual team members monthly, quarterly and yearly
- your yearly goals and objectives
- recognition of behaviors you want to see, those behaviors that help you along the road to your ambitious destination
- conversations about innovation, possibilities and new products or services

If you have not shared your big thinking in the past, the heat of the conversation is not the time to do it. But if you have shared these goals over time in many ways according to your plan, you can always tactfully reference them in the heat of the moment. You may quickly cover how it is important to achieve this goal, and therefore you are doing your best to make the current conversation successful.

Short-Term Thinking: Being Right & Being Emotional

The desire to be right might overshadow other aspirations you have of the long term.

Everyone has a strong desire to be right and to avoid the shame and anxiety of being wrong. It's not unusual then that you would want to appear right in each and every interaction in which you find yourself. Work situations seem to bring out an even stronger desire to be right than personal situations do.

> *The desire to be right might overshadow other aspirations you have of the long term.*

This may be because evaluation of your performance, your pay, your influence, your standing in the pecking order, your ability to get things done and your probability of promotion may be riding on your ability to do your job well. Therefore, looking wrong or incorrect in any situation could pose a problem. Many businesses have a culture where making a mistake is frowned upon or downright unacceptable. However, your ability to work with and positively influence others in your workplace could be much more valuable in the long run than being right in the short term.

▶ *Here's an example:* What you might really want to accomplish is to get a coworker to do their tasks in a timely manner, because the completion of these tasks supports your own work. Insisting they admit they are slow and have not been getting things done on time is not the best approach for long-term results. You could show data, point out what they are doing wrong and try to make them admit that they are indeed mistaken. However, this approach will most likely cause future resistance and unwillingness to work cooperatively. You see, it really doesn't matter if you are right; it only matters if they will do what you hope they will do. What you want to accomplish in the long term is what really matters.

Being short sighted comes from being scared in the present. If you often act out of emotion, you are acting for short-term gain or to avoid short term loss. In order to shift out of that mode of operation, you must consider your long-term goals in a conversation.

> *If you often act out of emotion, you are acting for short-term gain or to avoid short term loss.*

Your objective is to create ongoing productive conversations with those people critical to your success. Others can decide what type of conversations they want to have with you and if they want to speak with you at all. If, in all interactions, you have the long-term concerns of yourself and others in mind, it will become apparent, even if individual conversations do not appear to go well. If you wish to accomplish *your* long term goals, you must consider the other person's thoughts and feelings so they may decide to work with you.

Crucial Elements:

» Communication that simply communicates your point, with little regard for the integrity of the interaction can destroy relationships and wear out dedicated team members.

» Every conversation is either building or hurting the relationship with the person with whom you are conversing. Make no mistake, each and every conversation affects the relationship positively or negatively. The only acceptable responses from you are those that will strengthen this relationship if this person is in fact critical to your success.

» Over and over, expectations have been proven to determine results. This occurs because your beliefs and expectations determine how you act. It is human nature to not want to be wrong. Therefore, you will act in ways that make your beliefs and expectations true.

» When you Think Big, you realize results that are far above what you felt was realistic!

» The desire to be right might overshadow other aspirations you have of the long term if you are not consciously asking the question, "What do I really want to accomplish in the long term?"

» Being short sighted comes from being scared in the present. If you often act out of emotion, you are acting for short-term gain or to avoid short term loss. In order to shift out of that mode of operation, you must consider your long-term goals in a conversation.

6

**The Three Questions that can
Exponentially Improve your Business**
1. What do you really want to accomplish in the long term?
2. Where are they coming from?
3. How am I making them feel?

The Second Question:
Where Are They Coming From?

After you decide based on your goals and values what you want to happen in the long term and how that relates to your conversation today, then you can ask, "Where are they coming from?"

At this point, you consider how the other person could be thinking. You consider their frame of reference, what experiences they have been through and their history. It is only by getting to know them better that you can really hope to see things from their point of view.

Again you can think about Michael. He has been successful. He shares his vision and he is able to motivate his key players to achieve unprecedented success. Imagine the success he could experience if he was able to enlist the full participation of those on the team with whom he finds it harder to connect! What result that you are striving for makes it worth really getting to know your *whole* team and what makes them tick?

Good and Valid Reasons
The most important thing to remember is that wherever they are coming from, whatever they are thinking, *they are okay*

to think that way. There is *always a good and valid reason* why they are thinking how they are thinking, even if you would not agree nor do the same thing. However, this acceptance does not mean that their resulting behavior is appropriate or should be tolerated.

You cannot, nor should you try, to tell someone that what they are thinking is not okay. You need to meet them where they are, and understand things from their point of view. Then you are able to move together to a common destination that meets long-term goals and moves according to established business values.

> *There is always a good and valid reason why they are thinking how they are thinking, even if you would not agree nor do the same thing.*

You cannot just ignore the fact that where they are coming from may be foreign to you. You need to at least try to make sense of what they've said and the possible reasons why. You naturally assume, "I am right, and you are wrong." Why would you think any differently unless you have an unhealthy self-esteem? It is also natural for them to assume, "You are the problem."

> *You need to meet them where they are, understand things from their point of view.*

It will always take them longer to understand your side than their own and vice versa. It may take someone else longer to accomplish something than you or longer to process the conversation. You must remember that everything you think about from your point of view is easier for you to understand quickly than it is for anyone else.

Since it is natural for each person to see things from their own point of view, it is challenging to see a point that is different from yours especially if it appears to be in direct opposition.

Getting to Know Employees

Owners and managers should spend time getting to know their employees. I write that statement with reluctance, because socializing with employees for the sake of unwinding or trying to figure out how to help them with personal challenges is not the point of this time together. In fact, managers who forget where the lines of boss and employee are drawn could experience significant difficulties after inappropriate socialization.

Employees may become too familiar with the boss, start to treat them like a friend and treat their direction as suggestions. Personal information may be shared a bit too much to the point where the manager knows more than they professionally need to know about the employee. Once you know all the employee's challenges, it is harder to treat employees fairly and not give special treatment - like loaning money or giving an extra day off.

Not that you should not be concerned about employees' troubles, but the more you know the more you can be expected to help. It is not too much of an exaggeration to think that if you hear about one employee's struggles and bend the rules for them given the extremes of their situation, that you will then get the list of their challenges from other employees who also want accommodation. Each and every person could make a list of the hardships they face and ask for special treatment. There are always those as well who would never ask for special treatment, they may just quietly resign and work somewhere where the special treatment does not exist.

The fact is that in order to run a business well, you need employees to be at work, working hard, performing well and showing enthusiasm. When you listen and learn about employees, what makes them tick and a bit of where they are coming from, you can then help them to work more productively given whatever struggles they face outside of work or from their past.

The goal of getting to know the employees better is to communicate more effectively with them. The more you observe what is important to them, what experiences they have had in the past that have shaped who they are today and the stresses that have led them to where they are today, the more effectively you can respond to things that they do or say. This increases your tolerance and acceptance of why the employee acts the way they do and helps you realize there is a good and valid reason in their heads for how they act.

A Lifetime of Experiences

Each one of us has a lifetime of experiences that affect how we think, feel and act on a daily basis.

▶ *Here's an example:*

One of my most poignant personal stories occurred the first time my mother was diagnosed with cancer. Mom was never one for going to the doctor, so by the time she did, the "lump" she said she was going to have removed was Stage 3b breast cancer with a 90% chance of being in her liver and bones – a near death sentence. She had gone through the HMO channels and was scheduled to have surgery the following Tuesday. Working in health care myself, albeit long-term care, I talked to the nurses with whom I worked and explained the situation. They said she may not want to have surgery before chemo and that it was a terrible mistake the HMO had not involved an oncologist. They said she really needed to go to Roswell Park Cancer Institute – a local and very highly respected cancer hospital – for a second opinion.

I came home that day feeling as though I had done significant research, come up with great information and could not wait to share with Mom what I had learned and what we needed to do. I even had one of the nurses volunteer to call someone she knew at Roswell and try to get us an urgent appointment, which was almost unheard of since Roswell was always so booked. As I relayed this to Mom, I saw her wall go up. She was no longer listening and was not interested. She blatantly refused to go to Roswell under any circumstances, even if it meant imminent death. She was not interested in discussing the details. I reconfirmed with my contacts that this was a very important move – her chances of survival at Roswell as opposed to the HMO's suggested route were much greater.

When I pushed harder, my frightened and insistent mother told me that her father had died of lung cancer 40 years ago, very painfully, and she had watched him suffer at that same Roswell Park Cancer Institute. There was no way she was going through that! Roswell had been, and continues to be, on the forefront of cancer research. However, 40 years ago, cancer research was a much more uncertain area where if you really wanted a chance to live, you might try something dangerous, painful and torturous. She had watched her father suffer and die when she was 11 years old.

So, did Mom have a valid point? Of course! What did I want to accomplish? I wanted my mother to live! Where was she coming from? A frightening memory haunted her that led her to refuse to go to Roswell. At that point, I knew I had to realize the past experiences that affected her current decisions, to accept how she felt, and to give her refusal credibility before I could move forward to accomplish what I really wanted to accomplish – instead of telling her she was crazy for not going to Roswell.

Have you ever? Have you ever been in my mom's shoes? Maybe you were worried or scared to do something. Maybe you had a very real fear that others didn't seem to understand. Maybe you just wanted to ignore reality, regardless of the consequences. Have you ever been there?

Once we realized why she was refusing, as a family, we could then have delicate and supportive conversations that acknowledged those dreadful memories and still helped her to make a good decision.

As her daughter, I was sensitive to Mom's reaction, noticed when her wall went up and sensed her fear. I knew she was never scared of much, was generally open to others' suggestions and did not easily give up. That's why I didn't give up and continued to pursue the conversation in order to find out where she was coming from.

As a manager, you probably don't have the experience of a close relationship with your employees for the last 25 years. Therefore, it becomes even more important that you spend time getting to know your employees so you can observe when their walls go up, when they're worried or scared and when they feel tapped out.

Despite her fear, Mom was incredibly brave and agreed to an emergency appointment at Roswell scheduled the day before her surgery. Thank goodness Roswell had recently done a huge remodel, and we walked into a bright, cheerful, beautiful and welcoming hospital where the piano played in the front lobby. Mom was treated at Roswell, received the chemo before surgery, kicked the cancer and lived another eight years cancer-free!

You Learn When You Listen

It is not unusual in a situation like the one in my family for the person whom you fail to understand to not tell you exactly what the problem is. Often, their history and experiences involve emotions and therefore cannot always be discussed logically, nor presented in an easy-to-understand format.

Therefore, it's important that you become an avid listener and are able to ask good questions. In order to find out where others are coming from you have to listen. You have to ask questions and have a genuine interest in who they are and what their world looks like.

Listening Well

Even hard-charging, action-oriented individuals can be great listeners. However, the art of listening well does escape many fast-paced business owners and managers despite an intellectual understanding of its importance. Listening is an attitude about people and what they have to say. Are you a good listener?

When you listen well, you are truly interested in the words someone is saying, why they might be using those words and the message they are trying to communicate. It's very important to realize that if a person says something, it was important enough *to them* for them to say.

Listening is an attitude about people and what they have to say.

A good listener listens to understand instead of listening to think of what to say next. Truly attempt to understand where they are coming from, what they are saying, and what they are trying to communicate. Look at how they are saying what they are saying to get cues on where they are coming from.

A good listener listens to understand instead of listening to think of what to say next.

Temporarily hold off on action. If you want to act right away and fix everything, you may not wait to understand the whole situation. You'll try to fix a problem that doesn't exist or push to help with something that they don't care about. However, in general people like to help others to solve problems and like to offer solutions. Others may not be looking for answers and they may not want you to *do* anything. What you want to do and what they are hoping you'll do may not match at all.

Have you ever found yourself distracted while trying to listen? The mind processes at least four times faster than the average person speaks. It is difficult to tune that other 75% of your brain into listening to the person who is speaking. Are you busy thinking about what you want to say next while someone is speaking? Are you chomping at the bit to jump in and solve the problem for them?

> *What you want to do and what they are hoping you'll do may not match at all.*

People will stop talking if you cut them off. You are communicating that what you have to say is more important than what they have to say. Hold off on responding, judgment, placing blame or preparing an answer. If you don't, you may miss what they say and what they mean.

When you are a leader, people rightly come to you looking for you to take action especially if you have the experience, knowledge and other resources they may not have. There is a delicate balance between listening well and then acting because you are the right person to help them, and listening briefly and then acting because of your personal desire to be able to do something.

Demonstrate a Genuine Interest

A key to listening is to demonstrate a genuine interest in how people feel, what they think, what's important to them and what they are saying. You must convince yourself that you really want to hear the message they are trying to send. You cannot fake a genuine interest.

In order to have a genuine interest, it's important to remember that everyone has different priorities, life experiences and frames of reference. Another person's behavior is more often about them, what they are thinking and feeling and what's going on in their world, than it is about you! That means that if they do something you find offensive, counterproductive, or damaging to your business, in most cases, it was not done with the hope of accomplishing those results. Instead it was probably done or said based more on where they are coming from. This could be lack of knowledge, fear of repercussions, lack of confidence or different frame of reference.

Assumptions

Everyone makes some assumptions. Assumptions speed up your processes, and they are often harmless or helpful. However, you have to be careful you don't assume you know what they mean, what they are trying to communicate or assume agreement or disagreement with yourself.

 What assumptions do you routinely make when communicating with people in general or with a particular individual?

Since they are your assumptions, they can be hard for you to pinpoint. Dictionary.com defines assumption with these words:

1. something taken for granted;
2. the act of taking to or upon oneself.
3. the act of taking possession of something:
4. arrogance; presumption.

You have no right to make assumptions about what another person is trying to communicate. You need to spend the time learning about them and asking questions that you allow them to answer without assuming you know how they are thinking and feeling. As you read the definitions on page 82, you might see a dangerous possibility that you will make conclusions about what they are thinking and saying and take ownership of their thoughts. Then, you might act on your assumptions, not on their intentions.

Annoying Behaviors

Chances are there are things that people say and do that really annoy you – and may even cause you to get immediately angry. There may be things you really hate to hear people say, like "I can't," or "It's not my fault."

When you hear something that you dread, that you do not want to hear, and that annoys you, you may shut down and not pay attention to what someone is saying, what their words mean to them, and what they are really trying to communicate. You then lose your opportunity to enlist them to help you to reach your goals.

> *You then lose your opportunity to enlist them to help you to reach your goals.*

Observe yourself to see to what statements you react emotionally, take note of those, and ask yourself why these upset you. Be aware that when employees say them, you must pay extra attention to make sure you are really listening to the rest of what they say. Jot down a quick list of what you really hate to hear people say. Chances are there are also things that people do that automatically set you off, annoy you and may cause you to stop thinking positively about that person and not be able to listen. Add these to your list. Then be aware that when these particular situations or behaviors occur, you may lose your ability to listen and to communicate effectively.

▶ *Here's an example:* Personally, I have little patience for several annoying behaviors of others. One behavior that I never understood is the driver who weaves all over the road, doesn't use turn signals and overall just doesn't appear to take into account the other drivers on the road. My perspective changed one August evening in Buffalo, NY. I had just left the hospital from visiting my grandmother. Until a few days before, she was a vibrant woman, picking weeds for hours in her lush and expansive garden, making wonderful food for us all, and playing pinochle with me at least weekly. I had played pinochle with my grandmother since before I can remember. She'd never let me win, but she would forgive mistakes.

A few days prior, my grandmother had collapsed in church, had been brought to the hospital and they had diagnosed her with severe dementia, which I found hard to believe since she was sharp as a tack three days before. It turns out she'd had a stroke that took a few days to fully set in. That night I had been to see my grandmother and brought my pinochle cards. We started to play and I threw a heart. She paused and looked a little confused. I prompted, "Grama, throw a heart." She threw a spade. My heart sank into my toes. At 97, I guess I thought she would be there forever. My grandmother was slipping away before my very eyes.

That night driving home, I was distraught. I was not paying attention on the road. I switched lanes without looking or signaling. The driver I almost ran off the road was sympathetic, moved quickly and waved and smiled as he drove by. Thank goodness he gave me the benefit of the doubt. From that moment on, when I was annoyed by someone else's behavior, I began to think about, "Where are they coming from?" Not every bad driver on the road has a legitimate excuse, but at least I'm open to considering that they might have something serious going on in their life that is causing them to drive so distractedly.

Have you ever? Have you ever done something very out of character for you? Is it because your mind was very busy on other things? Have you ever been so emotionally charged, drained or distracted that you've done something that isn't safe, isn't nice or that hurts others?

There is always a good and valid reason why people are thinking how they are thinking, even if you would not agree nor do the same thing.

When you are faced with someone who says or does something that really steams you, consider why they are saying or doing what they are saying and doing. Make a list of phrases and a list of behaviors that really annoy you. Then think of *three* good and valid reasons for each of these behaviors or phrases. For example, people act differently when they are scared, they lack self-confidence, they think you're out to get them, or they strongly believe differently than you.

Even if you still find their behavior or phrases annoying or inappropriate, it helps to know where they're coming from and realize their behavior is valid based on *their* beliefs, history and current situation.

Deal Breakers

If you believe someone is egotistical, demanding, defensive, or procrastinating, are you able to accept that? Can you not try to change them and still create a successful interaction?

 Which of these qualities annoy you? Which annoy you to the point where you cannot create a successful interaction with this person? Review the list below and check the appropriate boxes.

I Believe Them to Be:	This Annoys Me	This Annoys Me to the Point where I Cannot Work with Them
Egotistical		
Demanding		
Defensive		
Procrastinating		
Competitive		
Impulsive		
Emotional		
Self-Promoting		
Pessimistic		
Suspicious		
Passive		

Possessive		
Complacent		
Critical		
Perfectionist		
Oversensitive		
Rude		
Aggressive		
Opinionated		
Rigid		
Stubborn		
Meek		
Unsure		
Aloof		
Fault-finding		
Spontaneous		
Obstinate		
Sarcastic		
Defiant		
Tactless		

When you ask the question, "Where are they coming from?" you must consider your personal level of patience. Do you care why people do what they do? What do you believe about people? Are you okay with the things you believe about human nature in general? If you believe that everyone is out to take care of themselves first, you will be right about the majority of people – this is a typical human outlook. However, not everyone acts on that innate desire every time. And it does not always mean that others are hurt in the process. Remember what you have decided you want to accomplish in the long run. What do they hope to accomplish? Are they thinking short term or long term?

Listening to Understand

As the owner or manager you have tremendous power and influence. People value your attention. Center and focus on the person who is speaking. You can communicate this attention by making eye contact, speaking warmly and smiling, nodding and making comments to acknowledge what they are saying.

Some challenges that you may face when listening to understand are:

- You assume you understand you know what people mean.
- You may fail to consider how what they're saying means to them.
- You will hear what you expect to hear. You will listen for things that match your experiences.
- You will tend to assume agreement with yourself.
- You feel you need to talk more to convince others to agree with you.
- If you hear someone say something that you really hate to hear, you shut down and do not listen to anything further.

At some point, it will be time for you to start speaking. However, don't be too anxious and overly ready to jump to speak the first time they take a breath.

> *Generally, the first time someone pauses when you are listening, they're probably not done.*

Everyone needs to take a moment to breathe, gather their thoughts, and phrase things just right. Generally, the first time someone pauses when you are listening, they're probably not done. Also, rarely the first problem someone presents to you is the real problem.

You must ask questions before you can deliver your message. Otherwise, your audience won't be listening. Questions keep them talking and clarify the situation. Your goal is to define the reason they are talking to you and to understand what they are really trying to communicate. This takes time, patience and persistence. However, you can be like many managers and owners whose success is limited despite their drive, determination and hard work because of their inability to communicate effectively with others. Or you can spend some time and set your focus and determination on the Opportunity Spaces™ and experience great results.

The Curiosity Quotient
What is your Curiosity Quotient? The Curiosity Quotient is how good you are at being curious.

You might wonder if curiosity stems from a particular personality trait or if it is a learned habit. There are people who naturally do many of the skills described in this book well. It may seem that they communicate well without even thinking. Curiosity comes naturally to some – and that may be part of their personality. However, being curious can also be learned.

The depth of a situation, especially one that includes people, is always significant. People are neither simple nor predictable.

In order to begin to understand people, you first have to want to look at the depth of the situation, and peel through the layers of complexity. You could become a psychologist, or you could just become more curious and that would serve you well enough.

As a results-oriented leader, when you become more curious, ask more questions, and are able to more effectively communicate with your team, you will be intrigued by the depth of situations. This can make curiosity a habit even if it is not part of your personality.

You can make curiosity a habit even if it is not part of your personality.

Learning to be Curious

You are now at the point when the other person has spoken, but it is not yet time for you to respond. It's important at this part in the listening process to be truly curious about where they are coming from.

➡ *Here's an example:* Think of something about which you are really curious. If you think about something you are genuinely curious about, a bunch of questions will come to mind. Personally, I find myself curious about the weather. For example, currently living in a tornado zone, I'm curious what makes a tornado form and wonder about its inner workings. Having lived in New Orleans when Hurricane Katrina hit, I'm curious what causes a hurricane to form and how it works. Once you've lived through one natural disaster in your town, you tend to get a bit more curious about how weather phenomena occur. I'm curious:

1. What are the weather conditions that make a tornado form?

2. How long do they usually stay formed?

3. Why do they say the sky is red when a tornado may be coming? What exactly does a tornado sky look like?

4. Why do the clouds, winds and temperature act the way they do?

5. Does a tornado really pick up everything in its path and hold it in its grasp?

6. What does a tornado sound like?

7. Is it at all safe to be a storm chaser like those you see on TV?

 Think of something you can get really curious about and make your list of questions.

Here's an example, Mr. Jameson came into the auto shop, already screaming about how long the repairs would take even before he found out what was wrong with his vehicle. He was rude to the clerk and the mechanic. He complained about how slow they were and how other shops were much quicker with his vehicle. He vowed never to come back!

Why was he acting this way? If the employees can take a moment to be curious they could come up with some scenarios about what might make him so difficult. Maybe he is not normally like this. Maybe he really is a good and kind person that has been pushed to his limits.

Two weeks later, Mr. Jameson stopped back into the auto shop and apologized for his behavior. He explained that his wife has just been rushed to the hospital. She was in the intensive care unit and they didn't know what was wrong with her. His car has broken down on the way to the hospital today and he was worried sick every moment he could not be at her side.

They had been married for 45 years and this was a sudden and unexpected health crisis.

Maybe the employees could not have come up with this particular scenario by being curious, but they could have imagined several different situations that Mr. Jameson might be facing that would make him act in this way. Even if he never came back to apologize, the scenarios they envisioned would help them to take good care of him despite his behavior. They could win a customer for life by taking great care of him!

Possibilities

 How many possibilities can you come up with for what is happening in the picture below? Make a list of all the things that could be occurring in this picture.

A few examples...

1. A waiter is explaining the night's specials

2. A manager is trying to mollify angry customers.

Did you come up with positive possibilities – did you see potential good in the situation? Or did you see strife and problems? There is nothing wrong with either interpretation. However, it is good to be aware of your tendencies. Know what you tend to see first in a situation, because the same thing may happen when you are curious in a situation in the workplace.

You may not consider yourself creative and may not be able to come up with many possible scenarios for what is happening in the picture on the left. Creativity is not having crazy ideas that hit you out of the blue. It is being able to see possibilities, combine realities and create opportunities. For the picture to the left, did you come up with a lot of possible situations? Or did you simply explain what was happening without considering more than one or two alternatives? Know that if you generated a decent number of possibilities, then you may tend to do the same when you are using curiosity to understand an individual important to you and your business. If you only see one or two possible scenarios, then when you are attempting to be curious in an interaction with another, you may miss their point of view, misinterpret their situation and see it as more simple than it is.

It's possible that ...

Think of an annoying behavior that is exhibited by one of your employees. Now come up with three good and valid possibilities for why they are doing what they are doing. A good and valid reason is simply a reason strong and sensible enough that it makes sense to them in that moment. It is based on what they believe, their experiences and their frame of reference.

Write three statements that begin with, "It's possible that..." Many mathematicians believe that there are at least six possible solutions to every problem. Challenge yourself to come up with six good and valid reasons for their behavior. Remember, the behavior may still be inappropriate or unacceptable. But, you are trying to understand where they are coming from. You are working to understand them first, and then to connect with them enough to influence their behavior.

> *You are working to understand them first, and then to connect with them enough to influence their behavior.*

Your Team

For people you interact with routinely, it is important to really get to know them. Keep notes mentally or on paper about key people on your team. Keep an inventory of their strengths, skills and idiosyncrasies. In order to interact effectively, keep any judgments away from this inventory. You simply need to observe how they are. Remember, what they think and how they feel are always okay. It is only the behaviors they exhibit as a result that can be the problem. If you are really not okay with the behaviors you see and you feel these are driven by a very different outlook than yours, maybe then they need to be removed from the team. But chances are, there will be a lot of people who are different from you, even quite different, and despite the differences, you can still build a strong relationship with them.

Once you've made the conscious decision to be curious, then it's time to ask some questions. Page 95 lists a few curiosity questions that might work for you. These must all be asked in the context of being curious and to gather more information. No judgments are made at this point, and no blame is being assigned. Be careful to ask questions only to gain insight and without any underlying messages. You are trying to clarify where they are coming from, not to make a point with the questions you ask.

> *You are not trying to make a point with the questions you ask.*

Curiosity Questions to Ask:

Any of these questions can seem like you are drilling them with questions if you are not genuinely interested and curious. If you are truly curious, it will come across in your expressions and tone.

- Can you be more specific?
- How long has this been happening?
- Can you give me an example?
- Tell me more about that.
- What specifically do you mean?
- Can you tell me what you mean when you say, "No"?
  - Ask for definitions, gently.
- Who else is involved in this situation?
- I'm concerned. Why do you think this is happening?
  - Here you use the power word "why" but begin with a statement that makes this sentence sound nurturing and conveys a genuine interest.
- Who were you hoping would do that?
- Where exactly is the problem?
- When did that problem start?
- By how much?
- What have you tried in the past?
- How is this affecting you?
- How frustrated are you, on a scale of one to ten?

- Really? What do you think is keeping you from achieving what you want in this area?
  - Just by adding, "in this area" you make sure they realize that you understand they are struggling in a particular area and are not a miserable failure overall.
- What do you think is the hardest part to implement?
  - Compare this question to, "What's so hard about that?" Choosing your words carefully is very important. The second question sounds more accusatory, even though the words themselves technically ask the same question.
- Ask "Why?" at least four times.
  - You must ask carefully since "Why" is a power word and can appear very accusatory. Ask in a nurturing way or ask careful questions that get you the answers to "Why?" without using that word. You want to adopt an attitude of true curiosity without blame or judgment.

Careful Paraphrasing

You may preface your response by repeating what the person you are speaking with has said to demonstrate you were listening. When you do, paraphrase carefully. You might say something like, "If I understand you correctly, you're saying that…," and then ask your curiosity questions.

The opening "If I understand you correctly…" is more effective than, "You mean…," "I know what you mean…" or "I know how you feel…." There is a common approach called, 'Feel, Felt, Found' – "I know how you feel, I've felt the same way, and here's what I've found." These statements tend to cause a defensive reaction since there is a good chance you don't know how they feel or what they really mean just yet.

You can use the 'Feel, Felt, Found' tool, but say it this way: "If I understand you correctly, you're saying that you feel….," "I have had an experience where I may have felt similarly...," "I'm not sure if you'd find this helpful, but what I found is...." This approach is based on the assumption that you don't know how anyone else feels, but you are letting them tell you if you are correct about how they are feeling and if your experience sounds at all like theirs.

Have you ever? When someone has said to you, "I know how you feel," have you ever been angered by that statement and felt that they certainly didn't have any idea how you really felt? When some has said, "I know what you mean," have you ever felt they were not really listening?

Imagine an employee who has been through a rough time personally with family illness, a car accident and family members out of work. This situation causes stress on this person. The stress they feel and how they react is based on who they are, how they tend to react to stress, the support they feel in their family and a lifetime of experiences that lead them to believe certain things about situations like these. To say to this person, "I know how you feel..." and to proceed to tell them about a situation in your life that you consider to be relevant may cause a negative reaction. Although you may have had a similar situation and sharing that may feel good and could build a bond between you two, chances are the employee would rather talk more about *their* challenging situations. They want to feel like you are thinking about them and what they are asking from you, instead of needing to comfort you in return because of your past challenges.

Too often, the workplace is more pleasant for the employee than their home life. Home and families tend to put stress on us, despite all their wonderful qualities, rewards and benefits. Therefore, in the workplace, the more you can create a comfortable, rewarding and understanding place where employees are genuinely listened to, the more employees will feel part of a team and will want to contribute positively to that team.

Rate Yourself

The next time you have an opportunity to listen to someone critical to your business success, ask yourself these questions and rate yourself. It is important that you consider this person to be important to your business success to ensure your desire to listen well.

	Not at all			Yes, Definitely!		
Am I genuinely interested?	1	2	3	4	5	6
Am I focusing solely on this person and what they are saying?	1	2	3	4	5	6
Am I able to hold off on forming solutions to their problem in my mind?	1	2	3	4	5	6
Am I keeping eye contact and smiling appropriately?	1	2	3	4	5	6
Have I asked questions that allow them to clarify the situation?	1	2	3	4	5	6
Have I paraphrased effectively and carefully?	1	2	3	4	5	6

Their Impact

You will tend to assume others' intentions based on the impact of their behaviors on you. In order to be willing to stop, listen and consider where they are coming from, you need to separate intention from impact. If you want to ensure your willingness to adopt a curious approach, you must realize that the impact their words or actions have on you is up to you and whether you let it bother you or not.

At times, people act and speak to try to get a reaction or make you upset. However, when you get emotional, you lose control of your ability to positively influence the situation. Just because you feel a certain way because of something someone did or said it doesn't mean they meant for you to feel that way. Both their reaction and your reaction are based on each of your values, experiences and beliefs.

> *When you get emotional, you lose control of your ability to positively influence the situation.*

Crucial Elements:

» Wherever they are coming from and whatever they are thinking, *they are okay to think that way.* There is *always a good and valid reason* why they are thinking how they are thinking, even if you would not agree nor do the same thing.

» You must ask effective and perceptive questions until you discover their good and valid reasons. Only by discovering these reasons can you hope to respond in a way that enlists their participation in achievement of your long term goals.

» After you meet them where they are and understand things from their point of view, then you are able to move together to a common destination that meets long-term goals and adheres to established business values.

» Listening is an attitude about people and what they have to say, and an openness about possibilities.

» A good listener listens to understand instead of listening to think of what to say next. People may not be looking for answers and they may not want you to *do* anything. What you want to do and what they are hoping you'll do may not match at all.

» When you hear something that you do not want to hear or that annoys you, you may shut down and not pay attention to what someone is saying, what their words mean to them, and what they are really trying to communicate. You then lose your opportunity to enlist them to help you to reach your goals.

» You must ask questions before you can deliver your message. Otherwise, your audience won't be listening.

» As a results-oriented leader, when you become more curious, ask more questions, and are able to more effectively communicate with your team, you will be intrigued by the depth of situations. This can make curiosity a habit even if it is not part of your personality.

» You are working to understand them first, and then to connect with them enough to influence their behavior.

» Curiosity Questions must all be asked in the context of being curious and to gather more information. No judgments are made and no blame is being assigned.

These questions are asked only to gain insight and without any underlying messages. You are trying to clarify where they are coming from, not to make a point with the questions you ask.

» When you get emotional, you lose control of your ability to positively influence the situation.

7

The Three Questions that can
Exponentially Improve your Business

1. What do you really want to accomplish in the long term?
2. Where are they coming from?
3. How am I making them feel?

The Third Question:
How Am I Making Them Feel?

Why Spend Your Time?

You're in business; you're not a psychologist. It may not seem important to productivity or bottom line profit to be curious about how people feel. However, Michael hit a solid and surprising wall when he disregarded this important component. You can achieve plenty of success without considering others feelings, but it will be only the tip of the iceberg of what you are capable of accomplishing. Bringing out the best in your team will enable you to achieve incredible success!

Bringing out Their Best

Just as you need to have a genuine interest in where people important to your business are coming from in order to have productive conversations with them, you must also care about how what you say will make them feel. When people feel good about themselves, they act with a higher degree of confidence. They are more willing to step out of their comfort zones and are more willing to work alongside someone who makes them feel confident.

Take Responsibility

It's up to you as the business owner or manager to take 100% responsibility for what happens as a result of your actions and for how people feel after an interaction with you.

Take 100% responsibility for what happens as a result of your actions and for how people feel after an interaction with you.

It doesn't mean that you are responsible for making them happy or shielding them from reality. It does mean that if these people are important to your organization, you'd better spend your energy ensuring *you react in a way that will bring out the best in them.* You either hired the person or built a relationship for a purpose, so it's up to you to help that person and that relationship grow.

Taking responsibility doesn't mean taking the blame. It means that because you are in the situation, you are contributing to it. It does not mean that you are to blame for their actions in particular. Everyone acts of their own free will and makes their own decisions in a situation. However, as manager or owner, you wield influence by what you do and say. As long as they work for you, they will respond to what you do. Poor behavior is not your fault. Desirable behavior is often triggered by the supportive things that you say and do to help people to feel good about themselves and act in the best possible way.

Success in using the Opportunity Space™ requires that you think people are important enough that you do not want to see them sad, unhappy, unduly stressed or scared. You cannot prevent people from feeling a certain way in response to a situation. But you can do and say things that help them to feel more positive, confident and happy after interacting with you.

They're Okay

Just like it's okay to think what they're thinking, *however they feel is okay, too.* There is *always a good and valid reason* why people are feeling the way they are feeling, even if you would not agree nor do the same thing.

> *Just like it's okay to think what they're thinking, however they feel is okay, too.*

Each person's perceptions create their reality. We each live in our own reality – the way we look at the world. People's feelings occur without conscious thought and stem from how they see the situation and others. How they react or cover up their own feelings will determine how they behave. And those behaviors could be a problem.

When you are faced with someone who says they feel a certain way that you really don't understand, consider why they might feel that way. Make a list of phrases that people use to describe how they are feeling that really annoy you. Then think of three good and valid reasons for each of these scenarios. You may still find their phrases or responses annoying or inappropriate. But it helps to know where they're coming from and realize their behavior is valid based on their beliefs, history and current situation.

If they said something, it was important enough *to them* to say. Therefore, if you want to build a good relationship, their words should be important enough for you to address as valid.

Even if what they say is an outlandish exaggeration like, "No one cares what I have to say!" which is for the most part not true in any situation, it is time to look for their message and consider how they feel. An exaggeration is often a cry for help or a complaint that no one is listening. They believe if they

> *If they said something, it was important enough to them to say.*

say something extreme, they might at least get the boss's attention. Once they have your attention, what you say and do is powerful.

 Have you ever said something inappropriate, untrue or downright crazy to get attention? Maybe an idea or problem you have is not getting addressed by the rest of the team? Maybe no one sees the challenge the way you do and they really don't want to hear about another problem. There are situations where you might feel it is appropriate to say something that will gain attention, even if it is not in character for you.

▶ *Here's an example:* At times, you may want to ignore the "No one cares…" statement and address whatever problem is at the root. For example Laura says, "No one cares what I have to say!" She makes this comment right after she made a suggestion that she immediately realized was not viable. Instead of her admitting she made a mistake, the fact that she felt ignored led her to make that attention-getting comment. She wanted to hear approval for her suggestions and feel she was important. She wants to believe she is okay, valued and appreciated, even if everything she suggests is not in that category. At that point, an effective response might be to acknowledge her suggestion (not her comment) and suggest it get written on the flipchart paper with the rest of the suggestions. Then ask that she clarifies the suggestion just a bit. That gives her some of the attention she is looking for after her impractical suggestion, as well as gives her the stage to retract or otherwise edit that suggestion and redeem herself. If she insists it is a good suggestion, agree to consider it along with the others when it comes time to make a decision. The impracticality can be addressed one-on-one at a later time. All along, you as the manager are not addressing the complaint that "No one cares!"

If you look at the other facts and realities and ignore how they feel because you think they should not feel that way or should change, you will probably hit an impassable brick wall.

If someone is nervous, scared, frustrated, mad or hurt, these are facts to take into consideration when responding. If you look at the other facts and realities and ignore how they feel because you think they should not feel that way or should change, you will probably hit an impassable brick wall. Every one has basic human needs to be understood, feel important and feel appreciated.

Individual Styles

Each of us has a certain style in interacting with others. You need to be aware of how you tend to react, what's generally important to you and in what situations you enjoy interacting with others. For example, you may enjoy 'excitement' in conversations or you may find 'drama' a distraction.

Each person is a unique individual who approaches and responds to life – their job, their tasks, their family, stress and pressure – differently. However, you may have noticed that certain people seem to gel with you and others drive you insane. Maybe no one drives you insane, and that's part of your uniqueness.

Your Growth Team

Let's say you are focused on aggressively growing your business, against all odds. Here are some possible members of your team, and their potential strengths and drawbacks:

George wants to know specifically where you want to grow the business, by how much and by when. He would like to be given his assignment without lengthy explanation or discussion and would prefer to not have to work with anyone else. And when he finishes this particular assignment (well done and on-time), he expects his work to be compared to others' performance, to be rewarded, to be able to delegate the follow-up details and to move on to the next assignment. Unfortunately, George will annoy people in the process, leave some in the dust and take all the credit.

Mark has some great ideas of how the company can grow. He wants to know when everyone can sit down together and talk about them – and he's bringing the refreshments. He's great at getting everyone excited about their roles in the initiative. Then, he'll plan the follow-up meeting to celebrate progress and pump everyone up to keep the momentum going. Unfortunately, Mark's discussions may never produce great results and although everyone's happy, you'll all cry together, too, when the company doesn't grow.

Kerry is comfortable with what you are doing right now and follows the system faithfully. He can see how the current system could use a little tweaking to produce more growth. During the meeting to discuss new initiatives, Kerry routinely volunteers to help and support others in the growth initiatives. When Kerry offers to help, everyone knows it will get done. Unfortunately, Kerry's not that driven to step out of his comfort zone to try something new, especially if he has to confront others about doing their part.

Michael feels it is important to gather all the data about how you are currently performing and what is currently working before you start talking about how to change. He researches, gathers and sends this detailed information to everyone before the meeting and asks everyone to review it so they can discuss it in detail. Of the ideas generated at the meeting, Michael takes notes and assigns someone to research and explore each of the possibilities. Unfortunately, if Michael's in charge, his level of analyzing may mean the business never implements any changes or the situation may change by the time he feels everyone understands it enough to make a move.

Which of these employees drives you crazy? Who is on your management team? With which of these people do you really enjoy working? Are you effective at harnessing the good in each of these people and working together to minimize the impact of their drawbacks?

Do you wish you had a whole team of one type? Do you wish you could get rid of one of these employees entirely? Sometimes you think you have the wrong person in your company, when really you just don't know how to manage them.

Most teams have all of the characters in the mix. Managing them well first means you need to understand *you*, and then you need to understand *them* – all while focusing on what you want to achieve. If this concept is a struggle for you, get some help, read the plethora

> *Sometimes you think you have the wrong person in your company, when really you just don't know how to manage them.*

of resources on behavior styles, and work with a coach on looking at your team and maximizing their performance. Do something to make sure it doesn't drive you crazy, your team functions well and your business grows!

If you are like George or Michael, you don't thrive on the people side of interactions and prefer the facts, the logic and the concrete problem solving. You may find this step of determining how others feel maddening. If you try to push through a conversation with logic and without acknowledging how they feel and the emotions that may be causing them to be unproductive at the moment, their unexpressed feelings will most likely make it impossible for them to listen to you. Realize if taking time to understand others is a change in behavior for you, that it could exhaust you, and each opportunity will be work. You can do it, but it will leave you more tired and you'll have to go recharge by being alone or getting something concrete done.

However, you also have the most to gain. You are most certainly hitting walls because of your lack of interest or inability to "figure people out." When you do, you'll see radical improvement in performance!

Have you ever? Have you ever had a conversation with someone who thought very differently from you about what needed to be done and how to do it? There are people who live by the phrase, "Done is better than perfect." Others absolutely cringe at the thought of accepting work that is less than perfection. At which end of this scale do you reside? Have you had a conversation with a person who was at the opposite end?

▶ *Here's an example:* Jack was a good salesperson. And it was important that Jim, his supervisor, understood his style in order to help him to be successful. Every so often, Jack would need to come in to Jim's office and complain, and complain, and complain. He got very loud and upset. "Do you know what happened? I ordered four compressors and only three came in!" He would rant and rave about his frustrations. Jim would pay close attention, patiently listen, nod his head and show his genuine concern for Jack's situation. Jack knew Jim was listening and that was important to him. Then, without even a comment from Jim, Jack would talk about an exciting new prospect, his plan for closing the deal and would excitedly get back to work.

Jim never did address those behaviors as inappropriate because he saw over time how important it was to Jack to have that time to vent and be listened to. Jack would later stop in and apologize for getting all crazy. Jim would accept the apology and pat Jack on the back for his most recent new customer.

Telling the Truth – Tactfully

You've decided that you're going to choose words and a way to communicate that will leave people feeling good about themselves. Then you must couple that with the truth. Make no mistake. Trying to help the other person feel good about themselves does not mean that you ever deviate from the truth.

You can speak the truth in different ways. You don't have to say, "That's crazy, we'd never do that here." Instead, you could say, "Hmm, that's interesting. I had not thought about that. Tell me a little more about how you think that would play out." Keep in mind, if what they suggest is not your first preference, you may have a hard time seeing a good idea other than yours. You may find a real gem of an idea you never expected! Asking a question or two may also help them to explore their own idea and decide it's not the best if that's the case. And it helps you to understand their idea better, find the good points and make them feel as if they have contributed, even if it wasn't a big contribution to the overall solution. And if you end up "wasting" a little time on a bad idea, the thinking they did and they resulting buy-in they demonstrate will be worth it.

> *You've decided that you're going to choose words and a way to communicate that will leave people feeling good about themselves. Then you must couple that with the truth.*

Instead of saying...	Try this phrase...
You're wrong.	I did not get that same impression... I might be missing something. Here's how I see it...
You made a big mistake.	Can you talk about what happened this morning? I'm concerned about the Smith order... I heard the meeting didn't go so well, what happened?

Have you ever? Have you ever had someone tell you something that really was true but it hurt because of the way they said it? Or maybe you just weren't ready to hear the truth yet? Or maybe you were just coming to the conclusion that you were wrong, but needed a few more minutes?

Watch the Reaction

Watch people important to your success when you speak – how do they react? Do they stiffen up? Do they stop talking? Do they look away and scowl? Do they make defensive statements? Do they respond argumentatively or attack you or what you've said? These are all good indications that what you said was not well received. Maybe something you said made them mad, or caused them to feel self-conscious, unimportant or unappreciated. Even if they were wrong, they don't deserve to be attacked or feel unimportant. And if they feel attacked because of something you said or did, chances are you won't achieve what you are trying to achieve, because they have probably stopped communicating with you.

Watching their reaction requires that you are observant. Not everyone is. Especially if you are moving at a fast pace, you may not slow down enough to see how others are reacting. Try practicing the skill. Next time you are at the mall or in a public place, take just 15 minutes to watch people. How do they react to others? Do they avoid interactions? Do they smile at people they pass? What are they doing with their hands? What expression is on their face? What might they be thinking?

It doesn't have to take a lot of time. Watch people as you walk through a parking lot, shop at the grocery store or have a beer at the local pub.

It's up to you to act and react in ways that bring out the best in others. Thinking back to previous interactions with those people important to your success gives you an indication of how what you say and do makes them feel. Observe them when you interact, listen to what they say, notice what they don't say and keep watch for their body language. Mostly, make sure you consider how what you say *might* make them feel, play it safe and say something supportive that makes them feel valued and important. Your chances are best they will respond positively.

Crucial Elements:

» It's up to you as the business owner or manager to take 100% responsibility for what happens as a result of your actions and for how people feel after an interaction with you. It doesn't mean that you are responsible for making them happy or shielding them from reality. It does mean that if these people are important to your organization, you'd better spend your energy ensuring *you react in a way that will bring out the best in them.*

» Just like it's okay to think what they're thinking, *however they feel is okay, too.* It does not mean they can behave badly on the job, only that they must feel okay about how they are feeling in order to accept any information you have to offer.

» There is *always a good and valid reason* why people are feeling the way they are feeling, even if you would not agree nor do the same thing.

» If they said something, it was important enough *to them* to say. Everything they say is a clue to how they are feeling and where they are coming from.

» Work to increase your effectiveness at harnessing the good in each of your employees and working together to minimize the impact of their drawbacks. Sometimes you think you have the wrong person in your company, when really you just don't know how to manage them.

» If you look at the other facts and realities and ignore how they feel because you think they should not feel that way or should change, you will probably hit an impassable brick wall.

» You must couple your communication designed to leave people feeling good about themselves with the truth. Trying to help the other person feel good about themselves does not mean that you ever deviate from the truth.

8

Stopping the Clock
Seize the Space

You must take the time to make good decisions.

In order to make good decisions in the Opportunity Spaces™, it takes concentration and practice. Even if you are able to ask The Three Questions well, you must be focused on success to the point where you are willing to give up something incredibly valuable – time. One of the biggest challenges to concentration is taking the time to step out of the moment to be able to think. Chances are you have arrived at the success you have achieved up to this point by working zealously. It goes against your grain to slow down.

However, the amazing payoff you will experience when you take just a few seconds to stop and ask The Three Questions that you now understand intellectually, will be well worth your time. It will enable you to strengthen the relationships with your team members to achieve results you thought were out of reach.

It is much easier to positively affect a relationship by communicating well the first time. If you fail to take a moment to concentrate on The Three Questions, and as a result do damage to an important relationship, you will live with that problem for a *long* time.

When you take these few seconds, it's almost as if you're freezing time. I call it stopping the clock. The more purposely you can use the first few seconds of the Opportunity Space™, the more effective you will be in the long run.

> *It is much easier to positively affect a relationship by communicating well the first time.*

You will only stop the clock if you decide you want to and make a conscious decision to do so. When you care about the situation, you may get emotional about what is happening, and if you don't stop the clock, you may not say or do what will help you the most. You may react before you think through the best response. In situations where you don't have a whole lot to gain or lose, you probably won't spend the energy to stop the clock.

Stopping the clock requires a conscious choice and very deliberate behaviors. Do it deliberately and routinely and watch your interactions increase exponentially in effectiveness. There are two components to Stopping the Clock. They are:

1. Make yourself stop and think before responding.
2. Do or say something to buy a little thinking time.

Have you ever?

Have you ever responded quickly and aggressively to someone and felt bad later? Have you every reacted emotionally, not thoughtfully, and had a very poor interaction? Have you ever stopped yourself, paused long enough to let yourself calm down, and reacted purposefully? And was your response different from your gut reaction?

Get yourself to stop and think because your success is on the line. Things you may find it helpful to think about:

> *Get yourself to stop and think because your success is on the line.*

1. Freezing time

2. Being a fly on the wall

3. Pretending you're an observer – pull yourself out of the situation for a few seconds and watch the interaction between you and the other person as if you were an observer.

4. Putting yourself in the other person's shoes

5. Thinking something positive about that person

6. Taking a deep breath

7. Picturing something relaxing or calming

8. Thinking of how a person you admire would look right now and how they'd respond

9. Repeating a phrase you find meditative, thoughtful or helpful

10. Thinking about what you can say or do to make this a moment you can be proud of

 Take a moment to circle the strategies above that you will try using in your Opportunity Spaces™ to get yourself to stop and think.

Sometimes you need a few seconds where the clock is stopped and you are able to think. What to do or say to buy a little thinking time:

- Ask for a few seconds by saying something like:
  - "Let me think about that for a minute," or

- "Tell me a little more about that/why you say that/what you mean."
- Ask clarifying questions:
  - "Can you help me understand why you've said that?"
- If there are obvious tensions and emotions, suggest taking an hour or a day break from the situation. Tell the person you need some time and that you'd like to think about what they've said. If you want to and do take longer than a day, you are procrastinating. Procrastinating is the way of the perfectionist, because the perfectionist waits until their thoughts and plan are perfect before proceeding. Often, it is too late to make an impact on the other person by that point.
- Excuse yourself for a drink of water or a trip to the restroom.
- Take a walk.
- Pray.
- Breathe deeply.
- Make a request like, "Let's get coffee or water and then continue this conversation."
- Look away, say "Hmmm…" and let yourself think.
- Allow the silence. Silence is okay and is shorter than it seems. Try this exercise. With a stopwatch, have someone else time five seconds while you sit in silence and then you do the same for them. When you are not the one timing, it may seem like a very short time. When they are staring at you waiting for you to say "time," it may seem like a very long time.

 Take a moment to circle the strategies above that you can use in your Opportunity Spaces™ to buy a little thinking time.

Emotions

The objective is to react thoughtfully and logically, not emotionally. Emotion clouds judgment and destroys effectiveness. When you're emotional, you lose your ability to act purposefully.

You must stop and realize the emotions you are feeling in that moment. Then, take these emotions into account and realize how they are affecting your current mood. Take the other person's feelings into account and react

> *Emotion clouds judgment and destroys effectiveness. When you're emotional, you lose your ability to act purposefully.*

only after thinking about how their and your feelings might be affecting their and your ability to interact.

Your Emotions

Do you have challenges with anger management? How do you generally react to conflict? How emotional are you? What types of situations make you emotional? When have you felt emotional in the last week? How about yesterday? Take an inventory one day or week and keep a log of when you become emotional. Ask yourself what just happened and what specifically about that situation made you emotional. Emotional doesn't necessarily mean that you lost your cool, maybe only that you felt anxious, worried, scared, and a bit out of control. You may not even have reacted, and no one else might have known. But if you feel that way, log it and get a good picture of what it is that makes *you* emotional.

Being effective in stopping the clock requires a desire to invest your time and your energy in the conversation. Being emotional may lead you to be less willing to spend your time and energy on a situation. But, in order to be successful, you must believe the conversation is not a waste of time. What is clear in your head is clear to you, but just because it makes sense to you doesn't mean it makes sense to the person with whom you are speaking. The message you are trying to communicate must take the lengthy journey from your head to your mouth in order to be communicated clearly to someone else – and vice versa. This can take some time and patience.

Even if you start with the best of intentions, the way the other person responds can lead you to become emotional. However, the way what they say makes you feel is not always how they intended to make you feel. And chances are it may not have put you in the correct frame of mind in which to respond in a way that helps you to accomplish what you desire in the long term. The more you are aware of when you are emotional, what triggers you to become emotional and what you need to do to regain your composure, the more effective you will be at using the Opportunity Space™ well.

Have you ever? Have you ever gone into a situation calmly and found your emotions spiraling out of control because of something someone else said or did? Are there individuals who trigger your emotions and your anger or frustration?

Regaining your Composure

When you become emotional, the conversation ceases to be productive. You will lose your cool. It is important to know what it is you need to do to regain your composure, come back to the person or the conversation, and once again be ready to be productive.

It may help to stop talking for a moment and take a deep breath. Or use the same strategies that worked for you to get yourself to stop and think (page 117).

When you become emotional, the conversation ceases to be productive.

It is also important to realize that what the other person says is much more often about them than you and personal attacks are usually self-defense and not well crafted responses. You may need to let a statement or two go unaddressed; knowing they were based on emotions and those particular points may not need any further discussion.

▶ *For example,* David complains that you, as the manager, are being unfair. If you honestly believe that you treat your employees fairly, ask him gently for an example. Then, consider his situation. You might realize that he is feeling a big lack of self confidence for some reason and by calling you unfair, he hopes you will back off. Maybe he has taken some personal time off and he feels guilty about missing work. Maybe there is a new skill he is having troubled learning. Possibly, he is accustomed to being the star employee, and a new employee is receiving a lot of attention for their talents. All these reasons are about him and have nothing to do with your fairness. However, if you like and respect David and take pride in being fair, his accusation of your unfairness could make you respond emotionally. *So first, realize his emotional accusation is most likely more about him than you.* Then, take a deep breath and get ready to respond unemotionally. Remember, an emotional accusation aimed at you is most likely about the person slinging it than it is about you!

Their Emotions

You must truly care about the feelings of the people with whom you're interacting. You will also benefit if you can get a reading into their feelings and what makes *them* emotional. A good way to do this is to observe their body language. Watch for noticeable changes in how they are acting that might indicate that you have said or done something that has interested or even offended them.

> Often, an emotional accusation aimed at you is most likely more about the person slinging it than it is about you!

You want to do your best to keep the conversation going – and if you have caused them to become emotional, a productive conversation may not occur. If they cross their arms, fail to make eye contact, scowl, grunt – all of these can be symbols that they do not wish to continue the conversation as it is presently going. If this is someone who you interact with on a regular basis, figure out what sets them off or makes them emotional, and then avoid it. Remember, when they become emotional, the conversation cannot be as productive and has a much smaller chance of achieving what you want to achieve in the long run.

Crucial Elements

» You must take the time to make good decisions.

» It is much easier to positively affect a relationship by communicating well the first time. If you fail to take a moment to concentrate on The Three Questions, and as a result do damage to an important relationship, you will live with that problem for a long time.

» Get yourself to stop and think because your success is on the line.

» Stopping the clock requires a conscious choice and very deliberate behaviors. Do it deliberately and routinely and watch your interactions increase exponentially in effectiveness.

» The objective is to react thoughtfully and logically, not emotionally. Emotion clouds judgment and destroys effectiveness. When you're emotional, you lose your ability to act purposefully.

» When you become emotional, the conversation ceases to be productive.

» Often, an emotional accusation aimed at you is most likely more about the person slinging it than it is about you!

9
Your Response

After defining your goals and values, thinking about what you want to accomplish in the longer term, considering where the important people in your world are coming from, and thinking about how they feel, it is *finally* time for you to react. As an action-oriented person who is focused on getting things done, this is the best part! It is time to interact with your team to improve the teamwork, tweak the processes, get everyone focused on success and enable even your "B" players to perform really well.

However, it is still a time to be cautious and use some of your precious time and energy to act purposefully. Be careful to avoid making personal accusations and attributing self-serving motives to people. Not only is it unproductive, but accusations always make another person defensive, and there cannot be a good conversation in that environment.

> *It is finally time for you to react.*

Powerful Words – Funnel the Power to your Goals
The words you choose can make a huge difference. Be aware of these powerful words and use them carefully and purposefully:

1. **No** – No stops people in their tracks. It puts up a wall. It closes down communication. Even if you disagree or feel the answer is "No," you can sometimes still answer "Yes" and clarify the conditions in your response.

▶ *An example:* The employee asks, "Can I have a $5/ hour raise?" You could say, "No way!" Or you could say, "I'm glad to see your drive. Here's what I would need to see in order to give you a raise of that size. You would need to increase your production by 200%, train new people in the position and be a leader on our annual project."

2. **Yes** – At the same time, "Yes" is extremely powerful as well. It makes people happy to talk to you. It opens doors. It opens communication. If there is any way you can be honest and forthright and say "Yes," do so.

▶ *An example:* "Yes, I'd be happy to look at that. Let's find 10 minutes next week," is much better than saying, "I'm too busy and can't look at that right now." That would cause them to feel unimportant, no matter how busy they know you are.

3. **You** – It's almost impossible to start a directive sentence with the word "You" without it feeling like you are pointing a finger.

▶ *An example:* "You need to fix that problem." Instead you might say, "I'd like to see you take on that challenge. Why don't you give it a try and if you're struggling come see me to ask me some questions."

4. **Why** – "Why" can be a pushy sort of word, even if you don't mean it to come across that way.

An example: If I asked you, "Where did you go to college?" You tell me where, and I ask, "Why?" You say, "Because I liked it there when I visited." I say, "Why?" Eventually, you start to feel as if I am being critical of your decisions. Use the other "W" words if at all possible to ask the same question, but in a less pushy way. "What made you decide to attend that college?" "When did you make a decision on which college to attend?" "Where else did you consider attending?"

5. **But** – When you put "but" in the middle of a sentence, you are usually saying that one half of the sentence is a lie.

  An example: "I really like that idea, but it won't work." "That's a great idea, but…" is essentially saying that it is not a good idea. Replace the "but" with a pause or an "and." "That's a great idea, and I'd like to explore the details a bit more, including the cost of implementation."

6. **Their name** – Everyone likes the sound of their own name. I realized the other day just how little I ever said my best friend's name. You tend to just talk if you are around someone a lot. Getting someone's attention by using their name is powerful and will start the conversation on a positive note.

Have you ever? Have you ever responded powerfully to one of these words? Maybe you bristled when someone told you "No!" or started a statement with the word "You." On the other hand, maybe you felt good when you heard the word, "Yes," or someone used your name when they were speaking with you. Who do you know who uses one or all of these power words often?

Keep a tally for a day to count the number of times you use each of these words. Put a hash mark below each word as you use it, notice the amount of power it has, and look at your frequency for the day. Maybe you will even stop, use the Opportunity Space™ and change from saying, "No" to saying, "Yes."

No	Yes!	You	Why	But	Names

Speak in Terms of Behaviors, not Adjectives

The idea is to have a productive conversation, not to personally attack the individual. Without realizing it, you often make statements that could be seen as an attack, like "You're grumpy," "You have a bad attitude," or "You don't have any initiative." You may feel that you are simply describing the situation, but you are using emotionally charged words to do so.

> *The idea is to have a productive conversation, not to personally attack the individual.*

The emotion comes from two places. It comes from you as the manager being annoyed or disappointed by the behaviors you see. It comes from the other person hearing these words that feel like a personal attack and becoming defensive and emotional. If you want someone to listen to what you are saying, state the problem in terms of the behaviors you have observed and without the descriptive adjectives. You can also state your feelings as facts and ask how the other person feels – as a matter of fact.

▶ *Here's an example:* Instead of "You're grumpy," it may be appropriate to say, "I haven't seen your smile in a while. I've noticed that when you smile and talk with the customers, they actually tend to purchase more products. Can you do those two things a bit more often?"

▶ *Here's an example:* Instead of "You don't have any initiative," it may be appropriate to say, "It's important to keep an eye on those shelves to make sure they are stocked. I'd like you to check on them at least every three hours and maintain the minimum stocking levels on the shelf. When are the most convenient times during your shift to do that?"

Many people are not accustomed to talking about how they feel. It is not common for people to have a deep introspective view of themselves. Quite simply, people in general are not in touch with how they feel, why they feel that way and why they react how they do. However, you are not trying to be their psychologist, you are only trying to determine a bit of what's going on inside their heads in order to interact with them most effectively.

> *Quite simply, people in general are not in touch with how they feel, why they feel that way and why they react how they do.*

▶ *Here's an example:* When I was finished pumping gas one day, "Clerk has receipt" came up on the pump's screen. At this particular station, it seems as if that message always appears. I did want a receipt, so I walked into the convenience store and asked the clerk for it. Then, I told her that the machine was often out of paper, requiring that I come in the building in order to get my receipt. Sometimes I have my children with me, and I didn't like to have to leave them in the car alone or do without a receipt. I suggested that maybe they could check the machines' paper supply just a bit more often.

She informed me that the machines were not out of paper, but that the customers pulled on the paper so much that the paper jammed. Well – those darn customers – always causing problems. So, I continued, determined to make my point. Then, maybe they should check more frequently for jams and clear them. She looked at me as if I were crazy. She said that it was the customers' fault, so all the customers would just have to deal with the problem. I just looked at her with disbelief and walked away.

I'm not sure if the other person in the store that day observing our conversation was her supervisor or not, but I can imagine the conversation that followed:

Supervisor – "You were really rude to that customer! Why do you always have to be so mean?"

Employee – "I'm not rude or mean! She was being unreasonable! I can't go out there every minute to check for jams – we're busy in here."

Supervisor – "Well you're just going to have to improve your attitude or you're going to have problems working here."

Employee – *Scowls*

That conversation did not go so well. The supervisor personally attacked the employee and used emotionally-charged words – "mean," "rude" and "always." The supervisor also used the vague phrase, "improve your attitude" instead of mentioning any specific undesirable behaviors.

Two Rules:

Tell the Truth.
Describe the Behaviors.

Tell the Truth.

Avoid saying "always" since this word rarely represents the full truth. The truth may be that an employee does something much more than you'd like, but then say that, and avoid "always" since it is untrue. Revisit the importance of telling the truth tactfully from Chapter 7.

Describe the Behaviors.

Describe the specific behavior(s) that you didn't like.

Let's try that again:

Supervisor – "That customer seemed pretty annoyed. What happened?"

Employee – "She was just mad that she had to come in here to get a receipt. It's no big deal."

Supervisor – "I'm concerned. It's really important that our customers are happy. There are so many other places they could go to get gas. Do you think there was a different way you could have handled that?"

Employee – "I guess I could have apologized for the paper being jammed and agreed that we could check it more often."

Supervisor – "That's a good idea. I'd rather see you suggest a solution. I wasn't real happy when your response to the customer appeared to place the blame for the problem on other customers. It's also a good idea to thank the customer for their suggestion."

Employee – "Ok, I will."

Now, you may not have complete buy-in from the employee at this point, but in this conversation, I feel like she was listening a lot better than she was in the first scenario. By starting out with "What happened?" you are asking the employee to describe the situation first, giving the supervisor the opportunity to see it through her eyes – valuable information to figure out where she is coming from and how she feels about it. Then, the supervisor reestablishes a store goal – to keep customers happy.

You and I Against the Problem

The feeling of this conversation puts the supervisor and the employee on the same side of the desk. They are solving a problem together in order to accomplish a company goal. Keep this visual in your mind.

Have you ever? Have you ever felt the difference between working with an employee to attack a problem together and the feeling that you were fighting the employee themselves? Which do you feel most often? Which is most productive for you?

Describing Behaviors:

In the exercise below, think of employees or those you know who you may describe with the words in the left-hand column. Review the example behaviors listed. Then think about the behaviors you see in your employees that lead you to describe them in this way. There are always observable behaviors that lead you to the conclusion that someone is mean, rude, lazy, etc. You must stop and think about what behavior you have observed.

There are always observable behaviors that lead you to the conclusion that someone is mean, rude, lazy, etc. You must stop and think about what behavior you have observed.

Instead of attacking the employee:	Describe their behavior:
You're rude! ie: Cutting others off mid-sentence	
You're mean! ie: Saying, "I don't care what you're faced with, here's all I can do."	

You're lazy! ie: Sees someone apparently struggling and does not jump up to help.	
You take no initiative! ie: Never brings a suggestion to staff meeting.	
You have a bad attitude ie: Often voices their concerns without any suggested solutions, doesn't listen to others' concerns and works on computer while others are speaking.	

What other adjectives would you use to describe your least effective employee?	Describe the specific behaviors they exhibit that cause you to describe them in this way:

Have you ever? Have you ever felt attacked by the words a peer, supervisor or employee has used to describe you? Did they appear to be attacking you instead of describing the situation and the specific things you did?

Desired Behaviors

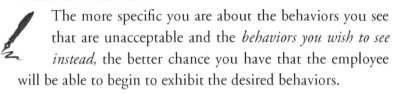
The more specific you are about the behaviors you see that are unacceptable and the *behaviors you wish to see instead,* the better chance you have that the employee will be able to begin to exhibit the desired behaviors.

What are the behaviors you wish to see instead?

▶ Instead of the *rude* behaviors you've described, you wish they would listen with genuine interest, make eye contact and ask at least one clarifying question.

Example of a desired behavior in your business:

_____

_____

▶ Instead of the *mean* behaviors you've described, you wish they would concentrate on making sure every word out of their mouth is positive, even if they believe they can't help. Ask questions to understand the situation better and find a way to help.

Example of a desired behavior in your business:

_____

_____

▶ Instead of the *lazy* behaviors you've described, you wish they would jump up and help if they see any indication that someone is struggling.

Example of a desired behavior in your business:

_____

_____

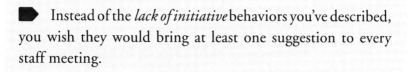 Instead of the *lack of initiative* behaviors you've described, you wish they would bring at least one suggestion to every staff meeting.

Example of a desired behavior in your business:

_____

_____

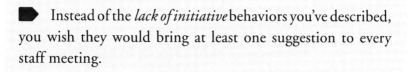 Instead of the *bad attitude* behaviors you've described, you wish they would focus on the person with whom they are speaking, voice a suggestion when they voice a concern, and ask others what concerns they have.

Example of a desired behavior in your business:

_____

_____

Don't let your impatience show through. If it is not natural for you to be so cautious and thoughtful, you may become worn out by this process of gathering information and asking questions to increase clarity. However, nonverbal communication is a huge part of successfully communicating, so it is important that when you do speak that you do not appear impatient. Take a second to take a deep breath, look at the person, and think positively about your response.

Don't give up! The results of your patient and purposeful actions will be worth every bit of aggravation and tiredness!

Sometimes what you want to accomplish is your sanity, and your goal is not to respond at all to what someone does. There are enough people who do things simply to get a reaction out of others. If you think someone is trying to get a rise out of you, then your objective is to not take the bait.

Choose your Battles

Once you have identified your goals and values, and explained the importance of doing things right, you must address violations. If you avoid those situations, you'll feel like your team doesn't care about what's important to you, has no loyalty to you and your company and may even be doing things wrong on purpose.

Discussing an issue will not always go smoothly. Few people look forward to confrontation, and at times addressing an issue head on can make things worse. But if you don't address the issue, things will certainly not get any better, and you rob the other person of the opportunity to change things. It's a tough choice.

No one is perfect. Everyone on your team is going to do things and say things that stray from your goals and values. Especially on small things, there will be battles you may not choose to fight.

If you don't address the issue, things will certainly not get any better, and you rob the other person of the opportunity to change things.

However, choosing to ignore a small deviation from your goals and values must be balanced with nipping problems in the bud early so that you don't send mixed messages that indicate certain behavior is okay.

▶ *Here's an example:* A common problem in meetings is the troublemaker who is overly negative, snippy, defensive or blaming. It may appear to be a small comment here or there and not something worth addressing. If one of your core values is to be a forward-looking, cohesive, problem-solving team, and you have explained the type of behaviors you expect to see, chances are this troublemaker is stepping outside the acceptable range – even if not by much. It would be best to first discuss this situation with the person in private, outside of the meeting.

You might take them aside and say, "I'm concerned about a couple comments you made in the meeting today and would like to take just a minute to discuss your point of view. When you said in front of Paul, "It's Paul's fault. He won't help me!" that is a conversation that maybe you and Paul should have had before the meeting, with me included if you need my assistance. It's really important to our company's success that we function as a cohesive team. I'd like to hear from you what's going on with Paul, but first, what made you feel like the meeting was the best place to bring that up?"

Some inappropriate behavior might be best addressed just before it happens again.

▶ *Here's an example:* If employees' reports are late, instead of spending time disciplining them or having a discussion, you may just want to reinforce the next deadline and talk about the task prior to the due date. If they are not on track to finish on time, talk about what they are planning to do to address the situation. This way, you are helping them fix a situation they may not have been able to fix without your assistance.

Smokescreens

A common mistake is when the owner or manager addresses the comment made by an employee rather than the fact that they made the comment in the first place. Unacceptable behavior is unacceptable behavior. Period. So treat it as such.

Too often managers fail to address a problem behavior and fail to hold the employee accountable. Instead, the employee presents a reason for their behavior which acts as a smokescreen. The reason becomes the subject of the discussion instead of their inappropriate behavior.

> *A common mistake is when the owner or manager addresses the comment made by an employee rather than the fact that they made the comment in the first place.*

Reasons are real, and there are always reasons the employee will present for their unacceptable behavior. And you may forgive an incident because of the reason, but you must still have the conversation about the behavior being unacceptable, and that it must not happen again.

If the behavior goes unaddressed and the reason is simply discussed, this may lead to a pattern of unacceptable behavior.

► *Here's an example:*

Employee is rude to a customer.

Supervisor (pulls employee aside) – "I'm concerned about the way you treated Mrs. Smith this morning."

Employee – "I'm so overwhelmed, I have a ton of things due today, and Bob isn't helping me."

(Warning! Smokescreen!)

The smokescreen works because it takes the supervisor off topic:

Supervisor – "Bob's not helping you - why not?"

Employee – "He has that other project he's working on, but I can't do this alone. He needs to be spending some time here with the customers, too. When I talked to him, he just gave me an attitude."

And on and on, the discussion of Bob - the reason and the smokescreen - continues and the unacceptable behavior goes unaddressed. The employee concern may be valid and the problem with Bob may need to be addressed, but the employee must also be held accountable for treating a customer rudely.

▶ *Here's the example again. The Supervisor is not taken off topic this time:*

Employee is rude to a customer.

Supervisor (pulls employee aside) – "I'm concerned about the way you treated Mrs. Smith this morning."

Employee – "I'm so overwhelmed, I have a ton of things due today, and Bob isn't helping me."

(Warning! Smokescreen!)

Supervisor – "Whew, it seems like you are quite frustrated at the moment. I'd like to help you work through that. First, we need to take just a moment to talk about what happened with Mrs. Smith."

Employee – "Well, she was being really demanding about what we promised we would get to her by yesterday. I told her it was only a day late and that I was really busy."

Supervisor – "It sounds like you may have dropped the ball. Our customers are the reason why we're successful, and we need to treat them like gold. It's important we meet deadlines, treat customers with respect, apologize when necessary and not burden them with any of our internal problems. How do you think you could have handled that situation differently?"

The employee is given an opportunity to share their point of view about the real issue – how they treated Mrs. Smith. Are you failing to address inappropriate behaviors or accepting smokescreens in your business or from your employees?

Haunting History

It may be challenging to address an unacceptable behavior if you have ignored it in the past. However, this is not a reason to continue to ignore the behavior. It may be difficult to defend yourself when an employee responds with, "Well, you never told me before that I shouldn't do that!" or "What's wrong with him today?"

If you decide to change the ground rules, it is important to bring that to everyone's attention. Point out that you have done things one way in the past and a few things need to be done differently from now on. Explain the new rules and why they are important. You don't have to justify yourself to your team. However, their buy-in will be more powerful if they understand why you are making changes. Make sure they not only understand your rationale, but also the consequences of failure to comply. Then, enforce the consequences.

When you explain the ground rules, the reasons and the consequences, employees are much more willing to work within these boundaries. "Pulling rank" and demanding certain behaviors just because you are the boss is rarely effective with the workforce that exists today.

Three Strikes

When you do not address an inappropriate behavior, be aware that after three strikes, you're out.

1. The first time an employee is rude to a coworker and you don't address it, they feel like they just got away with it. They may think that you didn't see what they did. The worst case is that they see you as someone whose authority they can ignore.

2. The second time they are rude to a coworker, they conclude that you don't care. They assume you must have seen the rudeness this time. In fact, they might be testing boundaries and have made sure they were rude where you could see them.

> *When you explain the ground rules, the reasons and the consequences, employees are much more willing to work within these boundaries.*

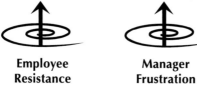

Employee Resistance   **Manager Frustration**

3. The third time they are rude to a coworker and you don't address it, they will assume you have condoned the behavior and will get defensive and resist if you try to address it later on.

Have you ever? Have you ever been surprised by the amount of resistance you saw in an employee on something you felt was logical and critical? Did you find yourself already frustrated that they weren't performing well in this area? Did your frustration coupled with their resistance cause a bigger problem?

Even if you have ignored a bad behavior in the past, address it now if it's an issue. If you get some comments from the employee about the "haunting history" where you have failed to address or even appeared to condone the behavior in the past, don't let it throw you off. If you are moving toward a bright future with solid core values, rely on those values to pull you through. You might say:

- I know we haven't talked about this much before. I have noticed lately how much this behavior seems to affect customer retention, so I think all of us need to focus on improving in this area.

- Sure, I've probably ignored this sort of thing to handle other fires in the past, and now is a really good time to start paying attention to this area with our big growth push in progress.

- This is an area where you really have not been focusing. I was just thinking about what a big impact it could have on delivery times if you increased the efficiency between your and Sally's departments.

Sarcasm and Humor

When you respond to people, sarcasm is never appropriate. You will lose credibility and may offend some people. It is always best to speak the truth. Use sincerity and say what you mean in a simple way that minimizes the chance that you will be misunderstood. Not to mention that sarcasm can be insulting! And no one wants to listen to what you have to say after you insult them. And you can injure your credibility if it is yourself you are insulting with the sarcasm. Often, the sarcasm will come back to bite you when you are misinterpreted, and it will be a long uphill battle to rebuild the trust, respect and responsiveness from others.

In fact, humor is rarely appropriate in serious work situations either. This is true because it is very rarely ever done well and there are too many potential pitfalls.

1. Humor is never appropriate at another person's expense. When humor is done poorly, it can affect many work relationships and be intimidating to others.
2. Self-deprecating humor can only hurt your credibility and others' image of you, even if only subconsciously.
3. Practical jokes are never appropriate since they have the potential to embarrass others, and cause friction and drama.
4. Work is a serious endeavor and people can easily get off track.

With all that being said, *it is good* to have a lighthearted workplace that occasionally has some comic relief for stress release and to keep the work flowing well. Just be aware that humor is very difficult to do well in the workplace and what might be funny to you may not be to others. And remember, that a relationship is much easier to maintain than to rebuild if broken down by a poor interaction.

Also, when you use the Opportunity Space™, you are hoping to have a very effective conversation and connect with the person important to your success. Humor and sarcasm have the potential to add confusion and to feel like a waste of time to those with whom you are speaking.

Disapproval

Emotional reactions to what someone does or says, such as anger, annoyance or impatience may cause someone to pay attention to you for the moment, but emotional displays will do little to contribute to a long-term working relationship.

Showing your disapproval is much more effective in influencing people's behavior than being annoyed at them. When your disapproval is based on set expectations, core values and what they "agreed" to, you are building a relationship by holding them accountable to those expectations.

Inherent in each employee's role are expectations that they will do the job they were hired to do. The underlying agreement must be there in order to have a successful working relationship. When you commit to using the Opportunity Space™ well, you must make the decision to express your disapproval and think about how to do that best.

First, bring up your disapproval without attacking them. Identify the unacceptable behaviors with an introductory sentence that doesn't start with "You…" Your statement should ask them to work with you, and encourage them to "sit on the same side of the desk" as you face the problem together. Two such introductory sentences are:

When your disapproval is based on set expectations and what they "agreed" to, you are building a relationship by holding them accountable to those expectations.

- I'm concerned about… because…
- Can we talk about…? It could become a problem because…

Then, it's time to get them talking. The more they talk and the more you listen, the better understanding you will have of where they are, where they are coming from and what it will take to connect with them in order to achieve what you hope to achieve in the long term. Also, the more they talk the more they will clarify the situation for themselves as they think it through.

Ask clarifying questions to ensure you are getting a full picture of the situation. Be aware if you are hearing symptoms or the real problem. When someone first reacts or approaches you, the real problem is rarely the problem they bring to you first. That's the power of clarifying questions.

Start your clarifying questions with opening statements in order to make people feel comfortable to open up and talk. You are not trying to get them to talk so you can "catch" them saying something wrong, you really do want to hear their version of what happened and need to communicate that openness to hear what they have to say.

Examples of opening statements:
- I get the impression that…
- I get the feeling that…
- I'd like to help…
- I'm concerned…
- I may be wrong…
- That's a good question/thought/observation…

Clarifying Questions

Be careful to ask questions only to gain insight and without any underlying messages. You are trying to get them to think and help you see the situation how they see it, not to make a point with the questions you ask.

- Ask, "What Happened?"
- Can you give me an example?
- Can you be more specific?
- Can you tell me more about that?
- I'm curious, why do you think that is happening?
  - Use "Why" only with a Softening Statement, such as "I'm curious…" Try to use "How" and "What" instead.
- Can you please define what you mean by [such and such]? Ask for definitions, gently. Don't assume you understand.
- Ask for their opinion. Restate the core value, goals, policy, or expectation that is important to you, and then ask them what they could do to meet that expectation.

If you wish to improve and employee's behavior and bring out the best in them, you must be willing to have the conversation that both shows your disapproval and gets them thinking. It is only when they have a trusting relationship with you and are using their knowledge and intelligence that they can produce the great results you expect.

Leading by Example

You are leading by example. How you react – what you say and do – sends a powerful message. What you do speaks much more loudly than what you say.

When you want to change the behavior of someone important to your success, first look at your own behavior. What do you do that could be leading them to act the way they are? Then consider what else you can do to model the behavior you want to see. This does not

> *How you react – what you say and do – sends a powerful message.*

mean you do their job for them, but there are parallel behaviors that you do as a manager to demonstrate what's important.

▶ *Here's an example:* When a customer makes an off-the-wall request, do you spend some time helping the employee to come up with a creative solution?

Desired Behavior: You may wish your employees were capable of handling off-the-wall requests creatively and diplomatically without your assistance.

You might lead by example in one of these ways:

- Employee asks for your help. It's a tough request, so you spend some time brainstorming for solutions with the employee.

- Employee asks for your help. You give them a few moments of your time and offer encouragement and convey confidence that you know they can handle it well. Give them your full attention, asking them a few thought-provoking questions to get them going. Then follow up later and reward desired behavior.

- A customer asks for you specifically, and you spend time with customer, being creative, diplomatic and introducing the employee as a capable team member to help them in your place should they need assistance in the future.

- Employees themselves make an off-the-wall request, and you spend time with them communicating creatively, honestly, genuinely and diplomatically and working to come up with a solution.

These are just a few of the ways your behaviors could encourage an employee to be creative, diplomatic and focused on the customer when a tough situation occurs.

When you don't react well
What happens when you don't react well? You *will* slip up at

some point. It will happen. You are not always going to read the other person well, know where they are coming from and have clear enough goals to guide you to say and do the perfect thing. Get up and dust yourself off. You can't give up! You can always go back and restart the conversation, apologize or clarify for mutual benefit. Remember Michael's plateau. Even if you own your own business and no one has told you you've hit a wall – think of what more you could accomplish with the intense loyalty, focused initiative and hard-charging performance that comes from a great team of people.

Crucial Elements

» **The idea is to have a productive conversation, not to personally attack the individual.**

» **The emotion in the conversation comes from two places. It comes from you as the manager being annoyed or disappointed by the behaviors you see. And it comes from the other person hearing these words that feel like a personal attack and becoming defensive and emotional.**

» **Many people are not accustomed to talking about how they feel. It is not common for people to have a deep introspective view of themselves. Quite simply, people in general are not in touch with how they feel, why they feel that way and why they react how they do.**

» **Observe the Two Rules: Tell the Truth. Describe the Behaviors.**

» **There are always observable behaviors that lead you to the conclusion that someone is mean, rude, lazy, etc. You must stop and think about what behavior you have observed.**

» **Discussing an issue will not always go smoothly. Few people look forward to confrontation, and at times addressing an issue head on can make things worse.**

But if you don't address the issue, things will certainly not get any better, and you rob the other person of the opportunity to change things. It's a tough choice.

» Beware of Smokescreens: A common mistake is when the owner or manager addresses the comment made by an employee rather than the fact that they made the comment in the first place.

» When you explain the ground rules, the reasons and the consequences, employees are much more willing to work within these boundaries.

» Showing your disapproval is much more effective in influencing people's behavior than being annoyed at them. When your disapproval is based on set expectations, core values and what they "agreed" to, you are building a relationship by holding them accountable to those expectations.

» You are leading by example. How you react – what you say and do – sends a powerful message. What you do speaks much more loudly than what you say.

10

Leadership and the Opportunity Space

Leadership is using influence, gained by developing powerful relationships, to motivate people to perform to their greatest potential to fulfill a shared purpose.
-Bridget M. DiCello

A manager makes sure things get done. A leader sets the direction and enables the employees to get done more than they ever thought possible and do it better than they imagined they could.

This understanding of leadership requires that you use the Opportunity Spaces™ strategically and are clearly able to answer The Three Questions.

Employees do more than they ever thought possible and do it better than they imagined they could.

A strong leader has a clear vision which creates a shared purpose for team members to work together to achieve. And the most effective leader is one whose vision and associated values and goals are clear to themselves, shared with their team and modeled by their personal behavior and actions. You may feel that you have a clear picture of what you are trying to accomplish, and the associated passion and a drive to turn that picture into reality based on hard work. But is your picture:

- defined enough to put it in writing?
- shared with your team so they are not surprised when you reference it as a reason to do things a certain way?
- modeled by not only what you do, but *how* you do business?

If your answers to the above questions are all "yes," then as a leader you have The First Question, "What do I want to accomplish in the long term?" under control.

Typically hard-charging, dedicated leaders are more effective with that first question than the next two. The leader, according to the definition above, also needs to use influence, gained by developing powerful relationships, to motivate members of their team. This is where the second and third questions come in:

- Where are they coming from? *and*
- How am I making them feel?

The only way to build the powerful relationships that allow you to have influence and to motivate others is to understand something about them, their frame of reference and how they react to you and to different situations. A boss

> *Understand something about them, their frame of reference and how they react to you and to different situations.*

and an employee always have the supervisor-direct report relationship. However, as the leader you know that in order to accomplish great things you must be able to count on your people to take initiative, learn something new, and push themselves to achieve more. In order for that to happen, you must build a powerful relationship with each employee.

The manager is responsible for getting the tasks done right. The leader is responsible for leading the team to achieve more than the team members ever thought they were capable of. The manager can find success by understanding the objectives, the tasks needed to get things done and by delegating duties and responsibilities. The leader must work to bring out the greatness in their team members in order to help each person discover their potential and contribute to the greatest degree possible to their vision and the shared purpose.

If you are currently the manager who gets things done right, but your team is not achieving to the level you feel they are capable or are not reaching the vision you see as possible, then you may need to more fully utilize the Opportunity Spaces™ that present themselves to you. When an employee says or does something you do not like, something that you feel they could have done better or does not perform to your expectation, be sure to ask the first question:

1. What do I really want to accomplish in the long term?

but also ask the second and third questions:

2. Where are they coming from? and
3. How am I making them feel?

to see if there is a way to understand the employee more fully and deepen your relationship with them, in order to access their full potential.

Crucial Elements

» Leadership is using influence, gained by developing powerful relationships, to motivate people to perform to their greatest potential to fulfill a shared purpose.

» A manager makes sure things get done. A leader sets the direction and enables the employees to get done more than they ever thought possible and do it better than they imagined they could.

» The only way to build the powerful relationships that allow you to have influence and to motivate others is to understand something about them, their frame of reference and how they react to you and to different situations.

11

Commitment, Practice & Recommitment

Using the Opportunity Space™ will enable you to take advantage of the multitude of opportunities that are available every day to make the most of the interactions you have with those important to your success. If you commit to implement the steps outlined in this book, you *will* become fluent at thinking through The Three Questions and responding well.

You will only chang if your return on your personal investment appears to provide enough improvement to make it worth your time and energy.

Commitment

What is your inspiration to change your behavior? You will only change if your return on your personal investment is clearly identified and appears to provide enough improvement to make it worth your time and energy.

Imagine the possibilities! You will have less turnover, your people will show more initiative and you will be able to spend your time on what you enjoy most instead of picking up the pieces of people who you would have otherwise left struggling.

You will experience greater business success, more effectively communicate your vision, increase the enthusiasm of your team and inspire greater respect and trust. You'll move one promotion closer to a senior management position, receive a compliment from that hard-to-please boss, and earn that top bonus. You'll experience less frustration when you interact with even difficult people, and decrease your stress about conflict situations, holding others accountable and delegating.

When you see people respond and change their behavior, act in ways you only dreamed possible, and do things they refused to do in the past – your business success will increase dramatically and you'll be sold on taking those Opportunity Space™ moments and using them faithfully!

It is much easier to act in a way that nurtures your important relationships than it is to try to repair one later. It takes a much greater amount of time to rebuild trust and credibility, but more self-control to do it right the first time.

> *It takes a much greater amount of time to rebuild trust and credibility, but more self-control to do it right the first time.*

Commit to use the Opportunity Spaces™ of the day based on what is currently frustrating you the most. Direct this frustration into spending the time and energy to implement practices that will help you to interact more successfully with your team.

In order to use the moment in between when someone says or does something and you respond, you must be effective at making decisions in those moments. It's important you go through the process to create written core values and goals for your organization or department. Then reference those to make good decisions and to answer The Three Questions well.

1. What do you really want to accomplish in the long term?
2. Where are they coming from?
3. How am I making them feel?

Choose a few strategies that will help you to stop the clock so you can expand those few seconds into thinking time. Embrace The Three Questions to the point where you will use them in a split-second during the day.

Teach the concept to your team and encourage them all to use them. Work though issues by using these questions with vendors, customers, subcontractors and others with whom your team may have conflicts. Challenge your team to think long term and to care as much as you do about the long-term goals and core values. Involve them in the clarifying process for those two areas.

How to Enact Change – Practice
After you've read this book, you will be capable of enacting a certain level of change just by reading the material.

When you hear something new, in order for you to really learn it, you must understand and practice it. The more senses you engage (eyes, ears, mouth, and hands) the more fully you can take in the material and the more change you can expect to experience.

Learning Steps

You need to enlist the help of additional resources. Based on your preferences, you might choose a respected peer, a mentor, a coach or a mastermind group to enact an even greater level of change than you can from simply reading the book.

> *You need to enlist the help of additional resources.*

1. **Exposure**

   First, you need to take in the information – often more than once. Do you prefer to hear it spoken? Read it? Or participate in a lively discussion?

2. **Understanding**

   Once you hear it, you must work to understand it. Do you prefer to read through scenarios? Discuss it with one other person? Or discuss it in a group?

3. **Practice**

   Once you've had a chance to think about it and discuss it, how do you like to debrief situations where you have practiced use of the concept? With a boss? With a coach or mentor? Or with a group? Do you prefer to lead that discussion? Maybe you'd rather be the teacher? You can learn a lot by teaching a topic.

4. **Accountability**

   Who is going to hold you accountable? Your method of communication is a challenging personal attribute to change. Without some outside accountability, chances are you will slip back into your old ways (since they have made you quite successful so far), and see the remaining challenges as having causes other than yourself. Accountability adds an additional level of commitment when you tell someone else what you will do.

When you use the Opportunity Space™, you will experience success. But then if you're like most people, you'll lose focus, it won't work a time or two and you'll get frustrated and want to stop. You'll need to make sure the first three steps of your learning process are strong and your accountability partner is determined and willing to work with you over a period of time.

As you continue to use the Opportunity Space™, you'll experience even more success, but then you'll get really busy, overwhelmed and in the craziness you will stop. Again, make sure there is a firm plan in place for Learning Steps one through three and that your outside accountability is a strong presence. The best thing a coach, boss or mentor can do is hold you accountable to what you have said is important to you, not accept excuses, and help you work through the reasons you are struggling.

> *Then you'll get really busy and overwhelmed and in the craziness you will stop.*

Practice using the Opportunity Spaces™ well and talk about successes and challenges. Recommit routinely to interacting well by continually assessing what is frustrating enough to make it worth your time, energy and focus to continue to refine your approach.

Once you experience the exponential impact of using the Opportunity Spaces™ well, spend concentrated time and energy formally teaching your employees how to do the same. Leading by example is very powerful, but doesn't always help them understand how to do it and how they personally need to approach a given situation. They also need time to absorb the information, understand it, practice it, and be held accountable. Follow steps one through four with your team as well.

Being a great leader can only get your company so far. You also need to teach and grow your team of people.

You will pay attention to what is being measured, by yourself or by someone else.

Measure Success:

You absolutely must measure your progress. You will pay attention to what is being measured, by yourself or by someone else.

Consider your inspiration to use the Opportunity Space™ (page 22). Then narrow it down to specific situations you wish to handle more effectively by behaving differently than you presently do. Then detail specific behaviors you wish others to stop or start, and what you wish others to do differently.

Track the number of times those situations occur, and put a hash mark on a chart like the one on page 160, when you or they handle it well. You may already be speaking to an employee about behaviors you want them

You will behave differently based on asking yourself The Three Questions in the Opportunity Space. This change on your part is expected to have a significant affect on their behaviors.

to stop or start. Measuring your progress is based on the premise that you will behave differently based on asking yourself The Three Questions in the Opportunity Space™. This change on *your* part is expected to have a significant affect on *their* behaviors.

My Specific Behavior that I do not like	Behavior I wish to exhibit	Successes on Mon.	Successes on Tues.	Successes on Wed.	Successes on Thurs.	Successes on Fri.
When an employee says "That won't work," I jump on them and say, "You're just lazy! You haven't even tried yet!"	My response is to take a deep breath and say, "Really? Tell me about your concerns," in order to get them talking and thinking of a good solution.					

Others' Specific Annoying Behavior	The Preferred Specific Behavior	Successes on Mon.	Successes on Tues.	Successes on Wed.	Successes on Thurs.	Successes on Fri.
Employees arrive at a meeting unprepared, let me lead it, and when I call on them, respond with "I'll have to get back to you on that."	Employee asks me two days prior what they need to bring to the meeting, asks clarifying questions if needed, and takes responsibility for a specific agenda item without me asking, presenting professionally in the meeting.					

Set a number at which point you will reward yourself. Yes, really. It doesn't matter if it is with a snickers bar, a new pair of sneakers or a day at the spa, there must be some reward for you when you reach a target number you have set. When you begin to see significant results, you won't "need" the reward because your business will grow significantly, your ambitious goals will be met, and your team will work together better than ever! Along the way, it's still important to track and reward yourself for your hard work as their leader.

By tracking the number of successes you have, you can not only track your progress, but also realize how often these challenging situations arise. If, as it does for many determined managers, it wears you out to interact with people and deal with the 'drama', then it is important to realize how frequently you are put in a tough spot. Commit to acting differently in order to decrease that frequency, but also realize how often you might either need to take a break to recharge or reward yourself in order to have the energy to keep going.

> *Take a break to recharge or reward yourself in order to have the energy to keep going.*

Crucial Elements:

» What is your inspiration to change your behavior? You will only change if your return on your personal investment is clearly identified and appears to provide enough improvement to make it worth your time and energy.

» It is much easier to act in a way that nurtures your important relationships than it is to try to repair one later. It takes a much greater amount of time to rebuild trust and credibility, but more self-control to do it right the first time.

» You need to enlist the help of additional resources. Based on your preferences, you might choose a respected peer, a mentor, coach or a mastermind group to enact an even greater level of change than you can from simply reading the book.

» As you continue to use the Opportunity Space™, you'll experience even more success, but then you'll get really busy and overwhelmed and in the craziness you will stop. The best thing a coach, boss or mentor can do is hold you accountable to what you have said is important to you, not accept excuses, and help you work through the reasons you are struggling.

» You absolutely must measure your progress. You will pay attention to what is being measured, by yourself or by someone else.

» Measuring your progress is based on the premise that you will behave differently when you ask yourself The Three Questions in the Opportunity Space™. This change on *your* part is expected to have a significant affect on *their* behaviors.

» Commit to acting differently in order to decrease how frequently unacceptable behaviors occur, but also to realize how often you might either need to take a break to recharge or reward yourself in order to have the energy to keep going.

EPILOGUE: OPPORTUNITY SPACES EVERYWHERE, EVERY MOMENT

Epilogue

Opportunity Spaces™ – Everywhere, Every Moment

The best way to do anything, whether climbing a mountain or eating an elephant, is one step at a time or one bite at a time (ewww!). Therefore, throughout your day, not only in response to what others say and do, but each and every moment is an Opportunity Space™ for you to decide what to do, how to spend your time, how you will think about a situation, and where you will focus.

Time Management

In fact, time management isn't even all that complex. To manage your time well, simply make the right decision every moment of every day.

> *To manage your time well, simply make the right decision every moment of every day.*

It's not easy to manage your time well, but it is simple. It is simple because you only have 24 hours in a day and no one can create more or slow it down, it just happens. What you can do is to very purposefully decide how to spend that time.

At Home

There are Opportunity Spaces™ at home as well as at work. Powerful relationships are not only the objective at work, but in your personal life. You naturally feel much closer to your family and friends than you might to your coworkers, and personal relationships are typically stronger than the relationships with those in the business world. Given that fact, they also have the potential to be exponentially stronger than any relationship at work. Where they are now could be only the tip of the iceberg! If you think you are happy now, just try using the Opportunity Spaces™ throughout the day with a spouse, child, or sibling! The results will be amazing.

> *How great your relationships are at home could be only the tip of the iceberg!*

Charity Work

Volunteering is a funny thing. People typically volunteer for something about which they are passionate. It doesn't even have to be something they are good at. Therefore, you end up at times with a team of volunteers with a wide range of personalities, a variety of skills and a bunch of passion. Sounds like a good team! Or it could be a difficult team with which to work. Typically, the passion trumps any trouble and lots of good work gets accomplished.

However, it might only be the tip of the iceberg of what is possible! Even if only a few volunteers use the Opportunity Spaces™ during their interactions with their fellow volunteers, a whole lot more could get done, get done well and best utilize the skills, personalities and passions of each person!

Living Purposefully

Using the Opportunity Space™ is living purposefully. Living purposefully maximizes your passions, determination, hard work, skills, talents, knowledge and drive. Whatever you have accomplished, no matter how great – there is more potential success. You have almost unlimited untapped potential as long as you can connect with others and build stronger and stronger relationships of trust.

About Bridget M. DiCello

Bridget DiCello is an expert in Customized Leadership Training and works with executive teams to exponentially increase their leadership abilities and company performance. She designs and delivers innovative, customized training sessions focused on solving real world business problems with solutions that can be implemented immediately. As a highly successful Executive Business Coach, Bridget works one-on-one with successful business owners and professionals across diverse industries. She has helped scores of business owners and managers analyze their business and refine their goals, and make changes that fundamentally and permanently improve their business. Her clients include members of the Fortune 100 companies and Inc Magazine's fastest growing companies.

Bridget is a sought-after speaker for conferences and company meetings and guest lecturer in prominent universities across multiple states. For nearly a decade prior to starting her own company in 2003, Bridget successfully worked in the management and administration of nursing homes and retirement communities and she holds licenses in Nursing Home Administration in California and New York. Bridget has been published in both professional journals and professional conference proceedings. She is a Certified Training Professional and holds an MBA with a concentration in leadership. She currently lives in Memphis with her husband Vince, their two children, their horse and their two dogs.

Bridget@BridgetDiCello.com | www.BridgetDiCello.com